Orbiting Ambition

orbiting ambition

The Anti-Burnout Blueprint for Lasting Success

Hunter Hess

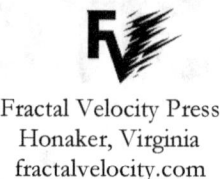

Fractal Velocity Press
Honaker, Virginia
fractalvelocity.com

© 2025 by Hunter Hess

ISBN 979-8-218-86150-6

orbitingambition.com

Contents

Introduction   **1**

1   The Problem with Linear Ambition   **5**

2   What is an Orbiting Ambition   **11**
The Impact of Your Orbiting Ambition   14
Finding Your Orbiting Ambition   18
Forming Your Orbiting Ambition   25

3   The Lunar Phase Framework for Success   **29**
The Physics of the Cycle: Why It Works   33
The Framework Unveiled: High-Level Flyover   36
The Lunar Cycle   40
Scaling Your Orbit: Side Hustle to Moonshot   42
Anticipating Gravitational Bumps   43
Your First Cycle: A Call to the Launchpad   45

4   The New Moon   **47**
Conducting Your Life Audit   49
The Art of Intentional Pruning   52
Untangling the Knot: Finding Root Causes   54
The Personal Mission Briefing   57
Defining Your Liberation Goal   60
Crafting Your SMART Goals   62
Overcoming Your Planning Biases   65
The Inversion Method   67
Assembling Your One-Page Mission Roadmap   69
The Ignition Test   70

5   Building Your Constellation of Skills   **73**
Skill-Building: Value Multiplication   75
The Skill Orbit: Understanding Your Constellation   77
The Skill Intersection: Where Your Skills Meet Needs   79
Intentional Skill Tracking and Development   82
The Rhythm of Progress   84

6   The Waxing Phases   **87**
Consistency: The Engine of Greatness   89
Systems for Achieving Consistency   91
Staying Consistent Through the Middle Stint   94
Discipline: The Principle That Keeps You On-Course   97
Discretion: The Art of Strategic Silence   100
Curating Your Inner Circle   102
"Walk the Walk" before "Talking the Talk"   104
The Three Pillars Working in Concert: Dyson   107

7   Managing Tidal Forces and Lunar Eclipses   **111**
Two Disruptors: Tidal Forces and Lunar Eclipses   113
Navigating Tidal Forces: Strategic Adjustment   115
The Pressure Valve Principle   119
Surviving Lunar Eclipses   122
The Physics of Recovery   126

8   The Full Moon   **129**
The Neurochemistry of Victory: Celebration Science   130
The Operator's Mindset   132
The Gravity of Success   136
Perils of the Peak: Two Shadows of the Full Moon   138
Reinvesting the Harvest: Fueling the Next Cycle   140

9   Mastering the Full Moon with Credibility   **143**
The Competence-Credibility Gap   146
The Three Layers of Reputation   147
The Network Effect   150
Building Reputation While Maintaining Integrity   153

10 The Waning Phases   **157**
The After-Action Review   160
Creating a Culture of Learning   165
The Deliberate Recharge   167
Active Rest: The Four Dimensions of Recovery   169
The Bridge to Renewal   173

11 When Reflection Reveals Revolution   **175**
　　The Signal vs. The Noise   179
　　The Pivot Decision Framework   181

12 Taking the Moonshot   **187**
　　The 3 Fears of Moonshots   189
　　The Ignition Moment   193
　　The Legacy Question   194
　　The Final Truth   195

Appendix   **197**
　　Acknowledgments   199
　　References and Notes   201
　　About the Author   207

orbiting ambition

Introduction

I wasn't thinking about success that night. I was just driving.

It was late, the kind of quiet stretch of highway where your mind starts to wander even as you keep your eyes on the road. The steady hum of the tires and the deep quiet of the night made everything feel still. I didn't think much of it; I was just driving with a friend, heading home.

Then we saw it. Above the dark horizon, hanging low and impossibly bright, was a supermoon.

It looked close enough to touch, enormous and bright, taking over the sky. For a moment, it felt like the world paused. The streetlights faded into the background. The trees, the road, and the mountains all seemed to lean toward the moon.

I slowed down without even thinking about it. As the road curved, for a few seconds it seemed like the moon was following me, almost guiding me forward. It was familiar, but not ordinary. It felt alive, like purpose you could actually see.

Then, just as suddenly as it appeared, it was gone.

Maybe it was the next turn, a ridge, or a cloud. I don't even remember what blocked it. But in an instant, the moon was gone, and I couldn't find it again.

I kept driving, hoping it would show up again, but it never did. Only darkness remained, along with the steady sound of the tires and the faint glow from the dashboard. I realized it would take some effort to find the moon again.

That moment stayed with me, because it was about more than just the moon. It was about the pattern of how something so bright and inspiring can disappear in an instant. Clarity can show up without warning, light up your world, and then vanish before you have a chance to follow it.

There's a force in life that often behaves this way: ambition.

For years, I'd been chasing that same kind of light: the rush of achievement, the clarity of progress, the temporary high of reaching a new goal. And every time, I thought I'd finally "found it." But just like that moon, the feeling eventually faded. The next turn came, the light shifted, and I was left wondering where it went.

I realized I wasn't chasing the wrong things. I was just moving in the wrong way. I kept trying to hold on to moments that were never meant to last forever.

That drive taught me something simple but important. The moon does not stop shining just because you cannot see it. It is still there, moving through its phases, just as we do.

We are not designed for constant brilliance. Instead, we thrive in rhythms; periods of creation, reflection, growth, and renewal. The real challenge isn't fading ambition; it's believing it should burn relentlessly.

Orbiting Ambition is not about working harder or moving faster. It is about finding your center, the thing that draws you forward, and learning how to move in step with it. It is about choosing balance over burnout, intention over intensity, and meaning over just staying busy. When you stop trying to hold on to every bright moment and instead move with the cycle, you find something important. Fulfillment is not found at the finish line. It is found in the movement of the journey itself.

This book is not about quick fixes or celebrating hustle culture. It is not meant to give you a burst of motivation that fades away. Instead, it is a framework, a practical guide to help you find your *Orbiting Ambition*, set big goals, and master the cycle of achievement that keeps you moving forward long after your first success.

In the pages ahead, you'll discover the difference between Linear Ambition and *Orbiting Ambition*, explore a framework called the *Lunar Phase Framework for Success*, and see how its principles can be applied through both personal stories and well-known examples. My goal is to help you use this framework to build the legacy you want to leave, even if you're still defining what your legacy should look like.

That is what *Orbiting Ambition* is about: finding your own rhythm and building a life that shines in the darkness, even when you cannot see the moon. You have already started your orbit; now it is time to understand it, strengthen it, and let it guide you toward the life you want to create.

①

The Problem with Linear Ambition

Before we dive into what it means to find your *Orbiting Ambition*, let's take a moment to look at the model that quietly shapes how most of us think about success. I call this model Linear Ambition. It's the straight path we're told to walk, the ladder we're encouraged to climb, and the myth that suggests happiness and fulfillment are waiting for us at the next milestone.

Think about it: from the moment you are born, you already have ambition. It's not the kind of ambition you read about in business books or hear about in motivational speeches. Instead, it's something much more basic and real. It's the drive to get what you need to survive: food, warmth, and comfort. This instinct is built into all of us, and it's where our journey begins.

From your very first breath, even before you have words or conscious thought, you know what you need to survive. You need food to quiet your hunger, warmth to protect you from the cold, and the gentle touch of a parent or caregiver to let you know you are safe.

You don't have the words to ask for what you need. You can't gesture or explain. Instead, you have one simple and powerful tool: you cry. That first cry is not a weakness; it's your first way of communicating your needs to the world. It's a clear signal that you are driven, even from the very start, to get your needs met.

This is ambition at its purest form: knowing what you need, and doing something to get it. Every person starts here, no matter where they are born or what their circumstances are. We all share these first needs, and the same drive to meet them. This simple force is the foundation for everything that comes next.

As you grow, your world quickly gets bigger. You notice new things like bright shiny toys, the majestic glow of a TV, and the laughter of other kids on the playground. With each new experience, your ambition shifts and grows. You start to want more toys, more time with your favorite shows, and more attention from the people around you. Your tastes and desires begin to take shape, and you start to notice what others have, too.

Then something shifts. You see another child playing with a shiny red truck, and suddenly, that truck is all you can think about. Just by seeing someone else with it, you realize you want it too.

That moment is important. It marks a turning point in how ambition works. Now, it's not just about what you need inside, it's about what you see others have. Your wants start to be shaped by the world around you, not just by your own needs.

This is not a personality flaw; it's a core feature of human psychology. We are social creatures who learn from each other, and that includes learning what things to value.

This pattern gets even stronger when you begin school. You join a bigger group, and your wants start to mirror the things you see around you. Maybe you wish for the popular clothes, the latest game, or the approval of certain friends. What started as a simple need now becomes a search for belonging and identity.

As we grow up, this pattern doesn't go away; it just changes shape. The shiny red truck turns into a new Cadillac. The cool sneakers become a job title. The wish to sit at the popular table becomes the drive to live in a certain neighborhood or send your kids to a certain school. Many of us spend years chasing bigger salaries, nicer houses, or more impressive vacations. We're told that money is the key to all of this, so it's easy to fall into the habit of making money our main goal.

This is the hidden trap of Linear Ambition. It's the belief that success is a straight path, and happiness is waiting for us at the end. We're told that if we follow the plan, climb the ladder, and check all the boxes, we'll finally arrive. But as you keep moving forward, happiness always seems just out of reach, and the finish line keeps moving.

Think about this scenario: you get the raise you wanted, feel jubilant when you get the news, and it feels great for a month or two.

Then, it just becomes your salary, and you're already thinking about the next raise, bonus, or promotion. In psychology, this phenomenon is called the hedonic treadmill, and while we'll all experience this at some point in our lives, continuing to follow it will likely never lead you to a life of true happiness.[1]

Think of an executive who spends thirty years of 80-hour workweeks clawing his way to the C-suite. He makes partner, gets the corner office, the seven-figure bonus, and the country club membership. He has won the game he set out to play. Yet he finds himself staring at the ceiling at 3 AM, feeling a terrifying emptiness inside. He spent his entire life climbing a ladder only to realize it was leaning against the wrong wall. He was so focused on the "what" that he never stopped to ask "why."

We see this trap play out even on the world's grandest stages. Consider the scene after Scottie Scheffler, the world's #1 golfer, sinks the winning putt to capture The Open championship in 2025. He hoists the Claret Jug, his wife and young child beside him on the 18th green, emulating the perfect picture of ultimate success. But then, behind the microphone at the press conference, comes a startling admission: the immense thrill of victory, he confesses, lasted only a few minutes.[2]

In that moment of raw honesty, he was describing the absolute peak of Linear Ambition: the precise moment the hedonic treadmill comes to a screeching halt. Scheffler gave voice to a truth few champions ever admit: a lifetime of work had been poured into a feeling that was breathtakingly brief. What mattered more, he told the world, was his family. He was discovering, in real-time, that while the championship was a goal he could achieve, his family was the gravitational center he orbited.

This isn't a rare story; in fact, it's something many successful people experience. This pattern is so common because it is supported by the stories and messages we constantly hear all around us that tell us we will find happiness at our next goal. These messages are so familiar that we often don't even notice them, yet they quietly shape how we think about success.

Take a moment and think about your own life. Ask yourself the following questions:

- Do you feel exhausted after achieving goals you thought would fulfill you?

- Are you already thinking about the "next thing" before celebrating the current win?

- Do you judge your worth by external markers (title, salary, house, car)?

- Does your definition of "enough" keep moving further away?

If so, you're caught in the Linear Ambition trap, and you likely have felt the way that Scheffler felt after achieving a monumental accomplishment in your own life. Let's explore a few trends in society that contribute to this thinking.

First, there's the glorification of "the grind." We are sold a vision of success that is synonymous with relentless, punishing work. "Hustle culture" tells us that sleep is for the weak, that weekends are for side hustles, and that every waking moment should be optimized for productivity.

At first glance, this might look like a recipe for success. But if you look closer, being busy can sometimes hide a lack of real purpose. When you don't have a clear reason driving you, the grind becomes the goal itself. You stay busy to avoid the quiet moments, because in that silence, a difficult question waits: What is all of this for?

The constant hustle can become a way to feel like you're moving forward, even if you haven't chosen a real destination. It's like running on a wheel; moving fast, but not actually getting anywhere.

Another trap is the idea of contingent happiness: the belief that you'll be happy once you reach the next goal.[3] Maybe you tell yourself, "I'll be happy when I get the promotion," or "I'll be happy when the mortgage is paid off." But as soon as you reach one milestone, the next one appears. Life turns into a list of things you have to do before you can finally be happy, but that moment always seems just out of reach.

This way of thinking can appear motivational, but the side-effect is that it can also steal your present. It turns today into just a stepping stone for tomorrow, a list of tasks to get through while you wait for happiness to arrive. Even when you reach your goal, you may find that the goalposts have already moved.

Finally, there's the toxic addiction to societal status. When we lack a strong, internal sense of purpose, we become desperate for external validation. We need the world to tell us that we are worthy, that we are successful, and that we are okay. And so, we use external markers as a proxy for our self-worth.

Our job title isn't just a description of what we do; it's a shorthand for our importance. The brand of car we drive isn't just a mode of transportation; it's a signal of our financial status. The square footage of our house becomes a measure of our value as a person. We become obsessed with collecting these proxies, these symbols of success, because we believe they will fill the void left by a lack of genuine purpose. But they never do. An external symbol can never solve an internal problem.

This is how ambition often works in our world today. Our natural instincts, combined with a culture that encourages us to want more, can keep us chasing goals that never truly satisfy. The only way to break free is to stop climbing the same ladder and start looking for a new way to define success.

This is where we must draw a distinction; the problem isn't ambition itself. The problem is the kind of ambition we've been taught to pursue. We need to trade the empty, linear chase for something more powerful, more meaningful, and infinitely more sustainable. Instead of chasing this never-ending ladder of Linear Ambition, we need to find our *Orbiting Ambition*. In the next chapter, we're going to dive into exactly how to find it.

②

What is an Orbiting Ambition?

Now that we've set aside the idea that growth is a straight line, it's time to build a model that actually works in real life. *Orbiting Ambition* is that model. Think of it as a strong center of gravity that draws your goals into alignment and keeps you moving forward, even when life throws you off-course.

An *Orbiting Ambition* isn't just another goal to check off your list. Instead, it's the deeper purpose that everything else in your life revolves around. This is your personal "why" for everything you do. It's the sun at the center of your solar system. The goals you set are like planets, each one pulled into orbit by the gravity of your core purpose.

As we said previously, working for the sake of work is unstable. Without a clear "why," you don't reap the benefits of doing the work. If you determine your *Orbiting Ambition*, however, your work revolves around a much larger mission, enabling you to think bigger, become more decisive, and see your plans fall into place before they actually happen.

For example, you might set a goal to get a promotion at work. That's a great goal, but on its own, it's just a task to complete. It doesn't have a deeper mission attached to it.

On the other hand, an *Orbiting Ambition* would be to establish a lifelong commitment to mentorship and leadership to empower others. When paired with the *Orbiting Ambition*, the goal of getting a promotion is simply one step in service of that larger purpose. When your actions are pulled into alignment by the gravitational force of an

Orbiting Ambition, your life gains a profound sense of coherence and meaning.

This isn't just a clever metaphor. It's a real shift in how you approach your life. Let's look at what makes an *Orbiting Ambition* different from just being an oversized goal, so you can spot the difference in your own journey:

First, think of your *Orbiting Ambition* as a direction, not a finish line. Linear ambition is all about reaching specific destinations, such as becoming a millionaire, landing a certain job title, or buying a dream house. But once you get there, you're often left wondering, "What now?" The map you used to get there no longer works, and you have to start all over again.

An *Orbiting Ambition* acts like a compass. It gives you a sense of direction; a true north you can follow, no matter where you are on your journey. Instead of focusing on becoming a millionaire, you focus on building habits and systems that give you financial freedom. Instead of chasing a job title, you focus on helping others grow. Instead of just wanting a beach house, you focus on creating a space where your family can connect and recharge.

This difference matters. A destination is something you reach, and then it's done. A direction, though, is something you can follow for your whole life. You're never finished growing, building, or helping others. Your compass keeps you moving forward, giving you energy and purpose no matter what milestones you hit along the way.

Second, a true *Orbiting Ambition* gives you energy rather than taking it away. Think about the things you do that leave you feeling more alive, even if they're hard work. On the other hand, some tasks drain you, even if they're easy. When you're working in line with your *Orbiting Ambition*, you'll notice that, over time, it fills you up and guides your emotions in a positive direction.

The work might still be challenging, but you can ask yourself: does this opportunity make me feel more energized or more drained? If it expands your energy, it's probably in line with your *Orbiting Ambition*. When you're heading in the right direction, even difficult work can leave you feeling stronger instead of exhausted.

Third, an *Orbiting Ambition* can withstand failure. If your only goal is "to launch a successful startup" and it doesn't work out, it can feel like everything is lost. But if your deeper purpose is "to create new solutions for tough problems," then a failed startup is just one step along the way. Even though it is expensive and painful, it's still just a lesson, not the end of your journey.

Even with a negative outcome as large as a failed startup, the *Orbiting Ambition* itself is untouched. It's bigger than any single outcome. This resilience is what allows people to endure incredible setbacks and come back stronger, because their core purpose was never tied to any single outcome.

The Impact of Your Orbiting Ambition

Now that we've looked at what makes up an *Orbiting Ambition* on the inside, let's talk about what it does on the outside. Many people miss this: finding your *Orbiting Ambition* isn't selfish. In fact, it's one of the best gifts you can give to the people around you.

When you're living with a clear purpose, you create a kind of gravity that pulls people together. You become the steady center for your friends, family, and coworkers. Your sense of direction helps others feel safe and supported, and it gives you the ability to help not just yourself, but everyone in your orbit.

Without a clear *Orbiting Ambition*, you can end up drifting like an asteroid, pulled in every direction by outside forces, be it your boss's mood, the news, social media, or whatever is happening around you. Life feels scattered and unpredictable, and instead of creating stability, you're just reacting to whatever comes your way.

Think about the direct impact this has on your inner circle. Consider a parent whose ambition is linear and extrinsic, such as having a goal of getting a big promotion. Their mood, their stress level, and their availability to their family become entirely dependent on the chaotic, external factors of their corporate life.

A bad meeting with their boss means a tense, distracted dinner at home. A looming deadline means canceled weekend plans. Their family is forced to live in a chaotic, unpredictable orbit around the whims of their career. The unspoken lesson the children learn is that love, attention, and stability are conditional upon professional success.

Now, contrast that with a parent whose *Orbiting Ambition* is intrinsic and purpose-driven. This parent is still ambitious and driven, but their emotional state is not dependent on their boss's approval. When they face a professional setback, it doesn't destabilize their core identity, because their core identity isn't tied to their job title.

This enables them to model resilience for their children in a real, tangible way. Their decisions are filtered through their ultimate purpose. They create a stable, predictable, and nurturing environment. Their family exists in the warmth of a steady sun, not in the path of chaos. This shows how even a highly professional *Orbiting Ambition*, when it's truly yours, has a profoundly positive impact on your familial legacy.

This ripple effect extends into your community and career. A leader in a company who is just chasing the next title or a bigger bonus manages through fear and pressure. As an effect of this, their team becomes a collection of mercenaries, loyal only to their own paychecks, ready to jump ship at the first better offer.

Meanwhile, a leader whose *Orbiting Ambition* is "to empower others to do their best work" leads from a place of service and inspiration, allowing them to create a culture of purpose. They attract and retain the best talent not because they pay the most, but because they offer a chance to be part of something meaningful. Their legacy isn't just in the numbers they hit, it's in the successful careers of the dozens of people they mentored and developed along the way.

When you have this kind of clarity, it becomes magnetic. You don't have to convince people to join you; instead, they're drawn to your purpose. Whether it's coworkers, friends, or new connections, you'll start to attract people who share your values and want to be part of what you're building.

Choosing your *Orbiting Ambition* isn't about putting yourself first; it's about serving others in the best way you can. This is how you shape your world and help others do the same. As you grow, you'll be able to support and inspire the people around you to make their own impact.

Let's make this real with some examples. For decades, the standard playbook in the business world was pure Linear Ambition: maximize shareholder value at all costs. The goal was to sell as much merchandise as possible to maximize profits. It was a simple, linear equation.

While making money is still the fundamental goal of a business, now there are many corporations who take the idea of Corporate Social Responsibility to heart and strive to make a difference in the communities they serve. Business has also become a method of sparking change for founders who seek to inspire change on a large scale.

Take the popular outdoor apparel company Patagonia, for example. Their founder, Yvon Chouinard, had a much larger ambition than making money from selling sweater vests. Instead, his *Orbiting Ambition* was to prove that it was possible to run a successful, profitable business while being a powerful force for environmental good. This central purpose became the unshakeable gravitational force for every single decision the company made, and has enabled Patagonia to become synonymous with environmental responsibility and outdoor recreation.

Take this, for example: when Patagonia realized that industrial cotton farming was an environmental disaster, they made the terrifying and incredibly expensive decision to switch their entire sportswear line to organic cotton, a move that could have easily bankrupted them in the early 1990s.[4]

In a world where "fast fashion" and consumerism prevailed, a decision like this made it much more difficult to compete on the basis of price. However, making decisions based on their *Orbiting Ambition* of "doing the right thing for the good of the environment" has enabled them to compete on a metric other than price: the intangible asset known as customer goodwill. By producing products in a method that is more durable, longer-lasting, and of higher quality, they are able to provide their end customers with a premium product that lasts, rather than ending up in a landfill after being worn a handful of times.

The company took their environmentally-friendly status even further by instituting advertising campaigns that discouraged over-consumerism, and also started a program to donate 1% of all sales, regardless of profitability, to environmental causes.[5]

Each of these decisions would be certifiably insane for a company whose only goal was short-term profit maximization. But for a company with an *Orbiting Ambition* grounded in environmental stewardship, they were the only logical choices to make in service of that mission. That powerful, authentic *Orbiting Ambition* is what built one of the most beloved, trusted, and ultimately profitable brands in the world.

Patagonia has shown that you don't have to choose between purpose and profit. By staying true to their mission, they've built long-term value and a legacy that goes far beyond any short-term gains. The impact that Yvon Chouinard and his team have made will last much longer than any single business decision.

Ultimately, your *Orbiting Ambition* is about the legacy you want to leave behind. It forces you to ask the big questions: What kind of impact do I want to have on the world? How do I want to be remembered? How do I want my contributions to influence the next generation?

For some, the answer is a professional legacy, where you may focus on building a company, a book of knowledge, or a cultural movement that will impact thousands, if not millions of people. For others, it's a familial legacy, where you'll focus on building a family, providing for their needs, and having the greatest impact imaginable on the people closest to you.

There's nothing wrong with either kind of legacy, as both are real measures of success. Many people want to blend the two, making a difference at work while also focusing on their family's well-being. You might want to contribute to a company or cause, or you might focus more on caring for your family as you move forward in your career.

Let me emphasize that there is no right or wrong answer to this question. There isn't an answer key that states whether one avenue is right or wrong for you; anyone who tells you that either method is the "one best way" is leading you astray from your heart.

It isn't important that you pick the "right" answer, but it is critical that you look introspectively and choose **your** answer. It's critical that you listen to yourself and focus your efforts on building a legacy that is authentically yours. Otherwise, you'll build the legacy that other people want you to build, and you'll spend your life working towards things that misalign with what you were truly meant to do.

Finding Your Orbiting Ambition

So, how do you find this elusive thing that we call an *Orbiting Ambition*? It is not a matter of invention, but of observation. Your *Orbiting Ambition* already exists within you; it is a constant and powerful presence like the moon in the night sky.

But just like the moon, your purpose can be hidden from view. It might be covered by the clouds of what others expect from you, or by your own doubts and fears. Your job isn't to create a new purpose, but to discover the one that's already there. This takes patience and a willingness to step back from the noise, let your mind settle, and look honestly at your own life. To start, ask yourself these three important questions:

Question 1: "What makes you forget to eat?"

This might sound like a strange or overly simplistic question, but it is the most direct path to identifying your innate passions and talents. What we're really talking about here is the psychological concept of a "flow state." You've felt it before: that magical state of being completely absorbed in an activity, so focused that the outside world seems to melt away. Your sense of time becomes distorted, and hours can feel like minutes. There's no room for self-consciousness or doubt; you are fully present and engaged in the task at hand. It's the feeling of being "in the zone."

This state isn't just a nice feeling; it's a powerful biological and psychological signal. A flow state typically occurs when a challenge you are facing is perfectly matched with your skill level. The task is not so easy that you become bored, and it's not so difficult that you become overwhelmed and anxious. It's in that perfect sweet spot where you are stretched just to the edge of your abilities. Your brain loves this. It rewards you with a cocktail of neurochemicals that create feelings of focus, creativity, and deep satisfaction.

Being in a flow state is a sign that you are engaged in an activity that is perfectly suited to your natural abilities and deepest interests. Linear Ambition often forces us to work against our nature, to grind away at tasks we find draining and unfulfilling for the promise of an external reward. Your flow states, on the other hand, are a map to your intrinsic motivation. They show you what you are built to do.

18

So how do you use this insight? You need to become a detective in your own life, searching for the moments that bring you the most joy. Let's walk through an exercise that will help you spot where you're at your best.

Exercise: Flow State Analysis

The Flow State Analysis is a simple way to find out what activities match your natural strengths. Grab a notebook or open a new document, and give yourself a few quiet minutes to focus on this exercise.

First, start with a brain dump. Your task is to list every single time in your life, from childhood to today, that you can remember being in a flow state. Try not to filter or judge the answers, but rather write everything that comes to mind. Some answers might seem more productive and others might seem like hobbies, but it doesn't matter.

"Building a complex financial model in Excel" is just as valid an answer as "playing guitar for three hours" or "spending a whole Saturday organizing the garage." Let the memories come and write them down in a rapid-fire list.

- Did you lose track of time building complex LEGO sets as a kid? Write it down.

- Do you get lost for hours writing some code to solve a technical problem? Write it down.

- Have you ever spent an entire evening planning a detailed vacation itinerary, "nerding out" on the logistics and possibilities? Write it down.

- What about deep, engaging conversations with a friend or family member where you feel completely connected and the world fades away? Write it down.

Next, look over your list. This is your raw data. Now, try to spot the patterns. Look beyond the surface and ask yourself: what was I really doing in those moments? What skill or action kept me so engaged?

- LEGO sets, financial models, and vacation itineraries might all point to a love of designing systems or solving complex puzzles.

- Playing guitar, writing a story, or cooking an elaborate meal might all point to a deep joy in creating or improvising.

- Organizing the garage, cleaning up a messy spreadsheet, or helping a friend untangle a difficult personal problem might all point to an innate talent for bringing order to chaos.

- Winning a video game tournament, closing a difficult sale, or navigating a tough negotiation might all point to a love of strategy and competition.

Then, go through your list and circle the verbs, the actions you were taking. You're looking for the common threads, the activities that always seem to put you in your element. Here's a personal example:

One of my first deep flow states came from a DJ business I started in high school. I could lose myself for hours arranging playlists in preparation for an event. It was never just about picking songs I liked; it was about architecting the perfect sequence. I was obsessed with how the energy of one song would blend into the next, how to build momentum, and how to design a system that would guide a crowd on a predictable emotional journey over the course of an evening. Time completely disappeared. When I analyzed it later, I realized the joy wasn't the music itself, but it was about designing an experience.

Years later, I found that same feeling in a completely different context: writing code. On the surface, what could be more different from a packed dance floor than staring at a screen, trying to solve a technical problem? Yet the feeling was identical. I would spend hours working through a script, researching functionality and libraries that would help solve issues, and fitting the pieces together until I had built an elegant tool that could drastically reduce manual effort for myself or my team.

When I looked at these two seemingly unrelated passions, the true common thread appeared. The playlist curation wasn't just about "playing music," and the coding wasn't just about "solving problems." Both were about my love for building elegant systems that create a positive outcome for others. Whether it was an emotional system for a party or a logical system for a workflow, the deep, satisfying joy came from the same core action: taking disparate elements and arranging them into a perfect, seamless whole that served others. That insight turned out to be a massive clue, a foundational piece of my own *Orbiting Ambition* that has run through everything I've accomplished since.

Question 2: "What makes you righteously pissed off?"

The second question might seem a little strange, but it's often the most powerful for finding your *Orbiting Ambition*. This is because the things that bother you the most can often point to the problems you're meant to help solve.

Let me be clear: I'm not talking about the petty, everyday annoyances that make you roll your eyes. I'm not talking about being angry that someone cut you off in traffic or that your coffee order was wrong. That kind of chronic, reactive anger is destructive. I'm talking about a different kind of anger. A righteous anger. A deep, persistent frustration that rises up when you see something in the world that violates your core values. It's the feeling you get when you see an injustice, a glaring inefficiency, a stupid, senseless problem, and you think to yourself, "This is just wrong. Someone has to do something about this."

That feeling isn't something to ignore or push away. It's a signal and a sign of what matters most to you. This kind of anger can be a powerful source of energy and motivation. While your joy shows you how you like to work, your righteous anger often points to what you're meant to work on.

Think about it. Nearly every great movement for positive change in history was started by someone who got righteously pissed off.

- Martin Luther King Jr. was righteously pissed off by racial injustice.

- Susan B. Anthony was righteously pissed off by the denial of women's right to vote.

- Yvon Chouinard, our example from before, was righteously pissed off by the way corporations were destroying the natural world he loved in the sole pursuit of profit.

Their anger didn't tear things down; instead, it built something new. It gave them focus, energy, and the strength to keep going when things got tough. Your anger can be a gift. It reveals what you care about most. If apathy is the enemy of ambition, then anger is its ally.

If you're not immediately sure about the things that make you "righteously pissed off," there is an exercise you can take that can help you identify these areas. It's what I call the "Frustration Investigation," and it works similarly to the methods of the Flow State Analysis.

Exercise: Frustration Investigation

Begin with the Frustration Inventory. Just like with the flow states, take a few minutes to create a raw, unfiltered list of the things that genuinely frustrate you on a deep level. What are the recurring problems that make you shake your head?

- Is it the way your industry is slow to adopt new, better technologies?
- Is it the lack of quality financial education for young people?
- Is it the way your local community lacks or neglects parks and public spaces?
- Is it the way talented people at your company are consistently overlooked due to office politics?
- Is it the spread of misinformation online?

Now, for each frustration, try flipping it around. Turn each negative into a positive mission statement. For example, if something frustrates you, ask yourself: what would it look like to solve this problem or make it better?

- "The industry is slow to adopt new technology" flips to a mission to "be a catalyst for innovation and drive progress."
- "Lack of financial education for young people" flips to a mission to "empower people to take control of their financial futures."
- "Neglected public parks" flips to a mission to "cultivate community pride and build beautiful shared spaces."
- "Talented people are overlooked" flips to a mission to "create systems of meritocracy and mentor hidden talent."

This exercise turns your list of complaints into a list of possible missions. Instead of just feeling frustrated, you now have a set of challenges you might be meant to tackle. This is where you start to see the problems you are meant to solve.

Question 3: "What Do You Want to be Known For?"

The last question shifts your focus from what's inside you to the impact you'll have on others, and from today to the future. It's about how you want to be remembered after you're gone.

Most people hear this question and think about achievements. But *Orbiting Ambition* goes deeper. It's not about your résumé, but rather about your character, your values, and the impact you have on others. A better way to ask is: what story do you want people to tell about you when you're gone?

Your résumé lists your accomplishments. Your legacy is the story people tell about who you were. This forces you to think beyond titles and bank accounts and to focus on your contribution from the perspective of the people whose lives you will have touched. Here's an exercise to help you think about your legacy productively:

Exercise: The Legacy Snapshot

Start with the Headline Test: imagine your life is over, and a respected publication is writing your obituary. They only have space for one short headline that sums up your life. What do you want it to say?

- Is it "John Smith, CEO of a Fortune 500 Company, Dies at 90"?
- Or is it "John Smith, Beloved Mentor Who Transformed Thousands of Lives, Dies at 90"?
- Is it "Jane Doe, Pioneer in Genetic Research"?
- Or is it "Jane Doe, the Unshakable Heart of Her Family and Community"?

There is no right answer, but the one you choose is a powerful clue to what you value most.

Now, make it even more personal. Picture your grandchild, years from now, telling their own child about you. When they're asked, "What was Grandma or Grandpa really like?" what story do you hope they share? What memory sums up who you truly were?

- Is it the story of the time you helped them build a difficult school project, and in doing so, taught them the value of persistence and creative problem-solving?
- Is it the story of the time you stood up for something you believed in at a town council meeting, even when your position was unpopular, teaching them about courage and integrity?
- Is it the story of how you always made everyone, from the CEO to the janitor, feel like the most important person in the room, teaching them about respect and humility?

Write that story down. The memory you choose will show you the values and qualities you most want to pass down.

Forming Your Orbiting Ambition

Once you've answered all three questions and finished the exercises, take a step back and look for the overlap. Where do your greatest joys, your strongest frustrations, and your hopes for your legacy come together? That's where your *Orbiting Ambition* lives. You might not have a perfect sentence right away; it could just be a few words like "leadership," "creativity," or "connection." Your next step is to start weaving these ideas into your own mission statement.

As you begin to get a sense of what your *Orbiting Ambition* might be, you will inevitably be confronted by a powerful force: fear. There is a deep-seated social fear in rejecting the clear, well-trodden path of Linear Ambition. If your current path aligns with your *Orbiting Ambition*, you may have already had to overcome this fear in making some of the life decisions that have brought you to this point. For many people, however, choosing to follow your *Orbiting Ambition* will require sacrifices and changes in your life that may seem counterintuitive to the path that you've been traveling thus far.

Because of that, others may feel as if you're "stepping off the ladder" of the path they expect for you. You may choose to take a different career path. You may choose to write a book. You may choose to take risks that you don't typically take. These sorts of things may cause others in your life to think you've gone mad. However, the reality is that our friends, your family, and colleagues simply do not understand the mission that you are seeking to accomplish.

Some people might see your choices as risky or strange. You need to be ready for that and stay confident in your own path. Their doubts are about their own beliefs, not about your journey. It's up to you to value your *Orbiting Ambition* greater than their approval.

You might also worry that you're not good enough to follow your *Orbiting Ambition*. Maybe you feel like you don't have the right skills or experience. Remember, your *Orbiting Ambition* isn't about who you are right now. Instead, it's about who you're becoming. The gap between where you are and where you want to be is your roadmap for growth.

Without a clear *Orbiting Ambition*, it's easy to drift through life, pulled in every direction by what others want from you. But once you find your central purpose, everything shifts. You have a way to make decisions, a steady source of motivation, and a true north to guide you regardless of what is happening around you.

The first step is to stop searching for answers outside yourself and start looking within. Try writing a first draft of your *Orbiting Ambition* Statement and put it somewhere you'll see every day, like your bathroom mirror. Read it each morning and ask yourself: does this feel right? Does it give you energy? Treat it as an experiment and see how it fits as you move through your days.

Finding your *Orbiting Ambition* is the single most important piece of work you will ever do. It is the prerequisite for a life of purpose, meaning, and deep, unshakable fulfillment. It is like finding your destination on a map. But a destination is useless if you don't have a vehicle to get you there, and a map to navigate the terrain.

In the next chapters, we'll build that vehicle together. We'll lay out the map and dive into a practical, cyclical system for turning your ambition into reality, called the *Lunar Phase Framework for Success*.

③

The Lunar Phase
Framework for Success

In the last chapter, we focused on finding our true direction. We moved past the constant pressure of Linear Ambition and began to uncover our own, genuine sense of purpose, which I call your *Orbiting Ambition*. This vision, your central 'why,' is like your North Star: it guides you, but it is only one part of the journey.

Even the clearest destination needs a way to get there and a plan for navigating the unexpected turns along the way. In this chapter, we'll explore the framework that helps you move from vision to reality, step by step.

But first, we need to talk about why the vehicles most people are using to travel along their journey of success are broken. Think about the most common approach to making a major life change: the New Year's resolution. It's a perfect case study in flawed design. On January 1st, fueled by a mix of holiday indulgence and a culturally-mandated sense of renewal, we make a bold, sweeping proclamation. "This is the year I'm going to get in the best shape of my life!"

We start with a massive burst of unsustainable energy. We buy a new gym membership, throw out all the junk food in our pantry, and commit to working out seven days a week. For a week, maybe two, we are unstoppable. But this all-or-nothing approach is highly susceptible to failure, as it leaves no room for the complexities of real life. One day, you have to work late and miss a gym session. The next, you're at a birthday party and you have a slice of cake.

When we approach change with a rigid, linear mindset, even a small slip can feel like a total failure. The internal monologue kicks in, and you tell yourself something like: "I've already messed up. Maybe I'll try again next week, or next month."

By February, the gym is empty again, and the life-changing resolution you set is dead. The only winner is Planet Fitness, who convinced you to sign up for a 1-year gym membership that you won't actually use, and you feel like you've failed at your resolution because you let your new routine or diet slip. The problem wasn't a lack of desire or a failure of willpower. The problem was a fundamentally flawed system. **The straight line is the enemy of progress**.

A similar kind of thinking once shaped the business world, too. For years, big projects were managed with what was called the Waterfall Model. Teams would spend months planning every detail from start to finish, laying out each step in a neat, orderly chart.[6] On paper, it looked impressive. In reality, it often didn't work as well as expected.

The challenge is that life (and business) rarely goes exactly as planned. Markets shift, new competitors emerge, and people's needs evolve over time. The Waterfall model was too rigid to keep up. Many projects followed the plan perfectly, only to find that by the time they finished, the world had moved on and their work was no longer needed.

Eventually, the most successful companies realized they needed a different approach: one that could bend and adapt as things changed. They developed a new way of working called Agile. Instead of creating a single, comprehensive plan, Agile teams work in short cycles called sprints, building and testing small parts of a project, then pausing to reflect on what worked and what could be improved.[7] This cycle of planning, doing, and learning helps them stay flexible and keep moving forward, even when things change.

The *Lunar Phase Framework for Success* brings this same spirit of flexibility to your own life. It borrows the principles that help innovative companies thrive and applies them to your personal goals. Instead of relying on rigid, all-or-nothing resolutions, this framework offers a resilient, cyclical approach that fits the ups and downs of real life.

Our lives don't follow neat charts or perfect plans. They are full of unexpected events, everyday stresses, and sudden challenges that can throw us off-course. A rigid, linear plan often falls apart when faced with these realities. A cyclical approach, on the other hand, can absorb these changes, help us learn from them, and adjust as needed.

But this shift from a linear to a cyclical model is more than just a productivity hack; it is a fundamental redefinition of success itself. To truly grasp its power, we must confront the most pervasive and damaging myth of modern ambition: the myth of arrival.

Our culture is obsessed with this myth. We treat our lives and careers as if we're climbing a massive mountain. The entire focus is on the summit: that one singular point in the future where we believe happiness, fulfillment, and peace await us. "I'll be happy *when* I sell my company." "I can finally relax *when* I make partner." "My life will be perfect *when* I retire."

The climb itself is viewed as a grueling necessity, a long, arduous task to be endured. The problem with this "mountain climber" mindset is what actually happens when people reach the summit.

There's a well-documented phenomenon in the startup world known as "post-exit depression.[8]" Entrepreneurs grind for a decade, sacrifice everything, and finally sell their company for a life-changing amount of money. They've reached the summit. Yet, within months, many report feeling lost, aimless, and deeply unhappy.

The struggle, the climb, and the process were what gave them purpose, not the arrival. The same is true for many Olympic athletes who experience a profound sense of emptiness after winning the gold medal they've dedicated their entire lives to achieving.[9]

The idea that happiness will arrive once you reach your destination is an illusion. When we treat success as a finish line, we set ourselves up for a brief moment of satisfaction, followed by emptiness. The *Lunar Phase Framework* invites you to shift from the mindset of a mountain climber to that of a gardener; someone who tends to their growth through ongoing cycles and seasons.

A gardener's work is ongoing. Life, for them, isn't about reaching a single harvest, but about moving through a series of seasons and cycles. The New Moon is like winter: quiet, thoughtful, a time for planning and preparing the soil. The Waxing Phases are spring and summer, when seeds are planted and tended. The Full Moon is the harvest, a time to enjoy the results of steady effort. The Waning Phases come after, as the gardener gathers what remains, returns nutrients to the earth, and reflects on what worked and what didn't, preparing for the next cycle.

A master gardener finds meaning in every part of the cycle. The quiet planning is just as rewarding as the harvest itself. This framework is meant to help you appreciate the whole process of growth, not just the end result. The Waning Phases, especially, are what sets this approach apart.

A mountain climber reaches the summit and is left asking, 'What now?' The gardener, on the other hand, knows that reflection and preparation for the next season are essential for future growth. This system encourages you to see success not as a single peak, but as the ongoing practice of planning, acting, improving, and renewing. In this way, your ambition becomes something you can sustain and enjoy throughout your life, not just in one brief moment at the top.

Nature itself teaches us this lesson. A tree doesn't reach its full height all at once; it grows in rings, year after year. There are times of quick growth and times of rest, and both are necessary for strength and resilience. The *Lunar Phase Framework* is designed to help you align your ambitions with this natural, sustainable rhythm, drawing on the steady and dependable cycle of the moon as your guide.

The Physics of the Cycle: Why It Works

Before we unveil the framework itself, it's crucial to understand why a cyclical approach is so effective. This isn't just a nice metaphor; it's a system designed to work with your brain's natural wiring, not against it. There's a deep psychological and neurological physics at play that makes this framework a powerful engine for motivation and progress.

First, let's talk about a theory we will refer to as the Dopamine Loop of Progress.[10] Dopamine is a neurotransmitter in your brain that is heavily associated with motivation and reward. When you anticipate or achieve a goal, your brain releases a hit of dopamine, which feels good and motivates you to repeat the behavior.

The problem with massive, linear goals (like a New Year's resolution to lose 50 pounds) is that the reward is impossibly far off. You might work hard for weeks and see only a slight improvement on the scale. The dopamine hit is too distant to keep you motivated through the daily grind.

The *Lunar Phase Framework* is built to work with your brain's natural need for regular rewards. Each cycle is a short, focused effort toward a clear goal, the Full Moon phase. When you finish a cycle and reach your goal, you experience a real sense of accomplishment. This creates a positive feedback loop: each small success gives you the motivation to start the next cycle.

As Harvard Business School professor Teresa Amabile discovered in her research, the single most powerful motivator at work is not money or recognition, but the feeling of making consistent, meaningful progress. She calls it "The Progress Principle.[11]" In the *Lunar Phase Framework*, we expand on this principle and create a well-defined system for manufacturing regular, meaningful progress in your life.

Second, the framework helps you achieve Cognitive Closure by defeating the Zeigarnik Effect.[12] Ever wonder why that one unfinished task at work nags at you all weekend, while you barely remember the ten tasks you actually completed? That's the Zeigarnik Effect, which is the psychological tendency for our brains to remain preoccupied with uncompleted tasks.[13]

These "open loops" consume a huge amount of our precious mental bandwidth, creating a constant, low-grade hum of stress. A linear approach to life often means having dozens of these open loops running at all times: the half-finished book project, the diet you're perpetually on, the business idea you've been vaguely "working on" for years.

Each Lunar Cycle gives you a chance to finish what you started. The Waning Phases, with their focus on review and reflection, helps you bring closure to one goal before you begin the next. This process frees up mental and emotional energy, so you can start your next cycle with a clear mind and renewed focus.

Finally, and most importantly, this system is designed to build **self-efficacy**. A concept from psychologist Albert Bandura, self-efficacy isn't just self-esteem or positive thinking; it's the deep, unshakable belief in your ability to execute the specific tasks required to achieve your goals.[14]

The distinction is crucial: self-esteem is your general sense of self-worth while self-efficacy is your belief in your capability. It's the quiet, internal confidence that you have what it takes to get the job done no matter what.

This belief isn't built by reciting affirmations in the mirror. It is forged in the fire of experience. It is built, brick by brick, through what Bandura called "mastery experiences." Every time you successfully complete a task, no matter how small, you provide your brain with concrete proof of your competence.

The *Lunar Phase Framework* is designed to create a steady stream of small wins and enhance your Self-Efficacy. By breaking down daunting goals into manageable steps, each completed action becomes another brick in a wall of earned confidence, creating a powerful upward spiral. Success builds a genuine belief in your abilities, and that belief fuels even greater success. In other words, **success brings more success**.

Every time you successfully complete a Lunar Cycle, no matter how small, you are having a mastery experience. You are providing your brain with concrete, undeniable proof that you are the kind of person who finishes what they start.

When you're just starting out, your self-efficacy might be low. That's why your first cycle should be reasonably achievable. Your goal isn't to change the world in 30 days; it's to have your first mastery experience.

With each cycle you complete, your confidence grows. Over time, your belief in yourself becomes something solid and reliable, not just wishful thinking. This deep sense of self-trust enables you to take on bigger goals. The *Lunar Phase Framework* isn't just about reaching milestones; it's about helping you transform your identity to align with your true *Orbiting Ambition*.

The Framework Unveiled: A High-Level Flyover

The *Lunar Phase Framework* comprises four distinct yet interconnected phases. Now, let's explore the architecture of this celestial machine phase-by-phase:

Phase 1: The New Moon

Every strong foundation starts with a plan. In the *Lunar Phase Framework*, this is the New Moon phase: a time of quiet and reflection, when the moon is hidden from view. This is your chance to step back, think carefully, and set your direction. The work you do here shapes everything that comes next. The goal is to find real clarity before you jump into action. Skipping this step is a common mistake, as it's easy to want to get started before you've truly thought things through.

The New Moon isn't just for daydreaming; it's for thoughtful, active planning. In this phase, you'll focus on three main tasks:

1. The first is conducting a life audit, where you take a clear-eyed look at your current reality, identifying both your strengths and the real, root-cause problems that are holding you back.

2. The second step is to take an inventory of your "unfair advantages," where you will catalog the unique skills, resources, and experiences you can leverage.

3. Finally, you'll use what you've learned to set a clear, achievable goal for the next 30, 60, or 90 days. Then, you'll break it down into a few specific, measurable steps that you can track and accomplish within your chosen timeframe.

Think of an entrepreneur who has a brilliant idea for a new app. If they skip the New Moon phase and jump straight into coding, they might spend six months and their life savings building a product that nobody actually wants.

The successful entrepreneur, however, lives in the New Moon first. They do the hard, unglamorous work of market research, customer interviews, and financial modeling. They create a detailed blueprint. By the time they write the first line of code, they are operating with a level of clarity and confidence that their impatient competitor lacks.

The New Moon phase is your chance to think strategically, not just reactively. This quiet, behind-the-scenes work is what sets you up for real success. It's where you find your direction and make sure you're ready for the journey ahead.

Phase 2: The Waxing Phases

After the quiet planning of the New Moon, it's time to take action. The Waxing Phases are when you start building momentum. This is where your ideas begin to take shape and become real.

This phase is about turning your plans into action, moving from ideas to steady steps forward. Here, consistency matters more than intensity. It's not about how fast you go, but about building a reliable routine and making real progress.

Three principles govern this part of the cycle: **Consistency**, **Discipline**, and **Discretion**.

- **Consistency** fuels compounding growth. The person who writes a single page each day ends the year with a book. The athlete who improves by one percent daily redefines their limits in a year's time. Steady execution matters more than bursts of motivation and inspiration.

- **Discipline** helps you stay on track. It's what gets you to show up, even when you'd rather take it easy, and helps you stay focused when distractions pop up. It's about choosing your purpose, even when comfort calls.

- **Discretion** means protecting your early progress. Not every idea is ready to be shared right away. In the beginning, it's important to guard your focus and let your work grow strong before inviting outside opinions.

The Waxing Phases aren't about rushing or making a splash. They are about building a steady routine, focusing on your work, and showing up each day. This quiet effort lays the groundwork for everything that comes next.

Phase 3: The Full Moon

The steady effort of the Waxing Phases leads to the Full Moon: the moment when your work shines brightest. This is when your project is launched, your book is finished, or your new habit has become part of who you are. It's the time when your efforts become visible and you can see the results of your hard work.

This is a time to celebrate. It's important to pause and recognize what you've accomplished. You've taken an idea from the quiet of the New Moon and turned it into something real. Taking time to appreciate your progress gives you the energy and motivation to keep moving forward in future cycles.

The Full Moon, however, is not the end of the journey. It is a new plateau, and it brings its own unique set of challenges. The work now shifts from building to performing and optimizing. If you've just launched a successful restaurant, the Full Moon is the period when you are working to stay fully booked every night. The challenge is no longer about creating the concept; it's about maintaining excellence at scale. It's about hiring and training staff, managing inventory, and ensuring that the 100th customer of the night has the same amazing experience as the first.

Navigating the Full Moon is about enjoying the fruits of your labor while actively solidifying your gains and defending against the new problems that success inevitably creates.

Phase 4: The Waning Phases

After every high point comes a time to pause and recover. Once the Full Moon has passed, the moon begins to fade from view. This is the Waning Phases, a time for review and renewal. This time is often overlooked, but it's essential for long-term, sustainable growth.

In our culture of relentless forward momentum, we are taught to leap from one achievement to the next without pausing to catch our breath. This is a recipe for burnout and, even worse, for repeating the same mistakes over and over again.

The Waning Phases are your chance to pause and reflect. It's like reviewing the highlights after a big game, looking back to see what worked and what could be improved. The goal isn't to dwell on what's over, but to gather insights and recharge for the next cycle. This phase has two main parts:

The first is a simple but profound process of **reflection**. Here, you must ask yourself and your team a series of honest questions: What was our original plan? What actually happened? What were the key factors that led to our successes? What were our biggest mistakes or failures, and what can we learn from them? This is not about blame; it's about extracting every ounce of learning from your experience so that you enter the next cycle smarter and more effective.

The second practice is taking time to **deliberately recharge**. High performance is not about working harder; it's about working smarter. And the smartest people understand that rest is not a luxury; it is a biological necessity for growth and development. Elite athletes know that muscle is not built in the gym while they are lifting weights; it is built during the period of rest and recovery after the workout. Your mind, your creativity, and your willpower work in the same way.

The Waning Phases are your built-in, non-negotiable time to step back, disconnect, and allow your system to recover and consolidate the gains you have made. Skipping this phase is the fastest path to burnout. Honoring it is the key to staying energized and fulfilled in the long run.

The Lunar Cycle

In **Figure 1** below, you'll see a graphic summarizing the mechanics of the *Lunar Phase Framework for Success*. Feel free to reference this throughout the book to keep track of your progress.

Figure 1: *The Lunar Phase Framework for Success*

Choosing Your Cycle Length

Now that we've discussed the *Lunar Phase Framework for Success*, let's explore the optimal length for your cycle. You could choose a 30, 60, or 90-day cycle based on your goals, or it could be even longer if needed.

A 30-Day Lunar Cycle is Best for:
- Your first 2-3 cycles where you're building the habits
- Testing a new skill or approach
- High-uncertainty experiments

A 60-Day Lunar Cycle is Best for:
- Building a small product or project
- Developing a new professional capability
- Most "standard" goals once you've experienced this methodology

A 90-Day (or longer) Lunar Cycle is Best for:
- Significant professional milestones
- Major life transitions
- Projects requiring deep expertise development

It is up to you to examine where you are and how sizable your goal is in order to determine the optimal timeline for you. It's okay to shift to a longer cycle if needed; the goal is simply to make progress.

Setting a realistic deadline that you can keep, however, is crucial to building your confidence in your ability to achieve your goals on a consistent basis. You should take some time to consider this as part of your goal-setting process.

Scaling Your Orbit: From Side Hustle to Moonshot

You may wonder how this framework applies to your most significant, long-term goals: the ones that take years or even a lifetime to achieve. The answer is that the *Lunar Phase Framework* works in layers. Just as the moon's cycle fits within the larger cycles of the earth and sun, your smaller cycles fit within your bigger ambitions.

Think of your journey as a set of nested cycles. Your biggest ambitions aren't reached in one leap; they're built from many smaller steps. For example, if your goal is to write a bestselling book, that's a long-term project made up of many smaller writing and editing cycles along the way. You can't do it all in a night or a weekend.

To make it manageable, you break it down. Your goal for the year might be to write and edit a 60,000-word manuscript. This is still a big challenge, but it's much more specific and achievable than simply aiming to be a bestselling author.

Even a 60,000-word manuscript can feel overwhelming, so you break it down further. Maybe your goal for the next three months is to finish the first three chapters. Now, the task feels more approachable.

You can continue breaking your goal into smaller cycles, such as setting a monthly goal to write a draft of Chapter 2. Each step builds on the last, making steady progress toward your bigger dream.

Through the weekly execution of your Waxing Phases, you'll be able to work towards smaller goals that contribute to your larger goals. Your goal for this week may be to write 2,500 words and finalize the research for the next section. This style of work fosters consistency, enables you to celebrate both large and small wins, and encourages you to continue working towards a much larger goal.

Big, intimidating goals become manageable when you break them into connected, achievable steps. Each small action you take each week adds up to your monthly, quarterly, and yearly progress, all moving you closer to achieving your life's *Orbiting Ambition*. The structure of the *Lunar Phase Framework* enables you to see a much clearer path towards achieving the moonshot-level goals you seek to achieve.

Anticipating Gravitational Bumps

Any system is only as helpful as your ability to stick with it. As you begin your own cycles, you'll likely run into some common challenges. Knowing about them ahead of time can help you navigate them more easily. Here are a few examples, along with some simple solutions:

1. The Over-Ambitious First Cycle

The most common mistake is trying to change everything at once. Your first mission becomes "to lose 50 pounds, write a novel, and start a business." This is a recipe for overwhelming yourself and failing at all your goals due to a lack of a single, focused objective.

The Solution: start small. For your first cycle, choose one main goal and maybe one or two small, related habits. The aim isn't to change your whole life in 90 days, but to show yourself that the system works and to build momentum for the future.

2. The Perfection Trap

This happens when you get stuck in endless planning during the New Moon phase, spending weeks researching, organizing, and perfecting your system instead of actually starting. It can feel productive, but it's really just another way to put off taking action.

The Solution: favor action over endless preparation. Set a short, clear deadline for your New Moon phase; perhaps just a few days or a week. Remember, it's better to start with a good plan now than to wait forever for the perfect one.

3. The All-or-Nothing Mindset

This is the old New Year's resolution mindset showing up again. You're making progress, then life gets in the way and you miss a day. Suddenly, it feels like you've failed and you might as well give up.

The Solution: use the "Never Miss Twice" rule. Anyone can miss once, as life is unpredictable. The key is not to let one missed day turn into two, then three, and then a return to your old habits. The cycle is resilient. Get back on track the very next day.

4. Skipping the Waning Phases

This is the cardinal sin of high achievers. You finish one project, and the excitement and anxiety of what's next immediately pull you directly into the next New Moon phase. You skip the reflection and the rest. This is how you burn out and continue to make the same mistakes.

The Solution: Schedule your Waning Phases. Treat your review and your deliberate recharge time as non-negotiable appointments on your calendar. They are not a break from the work; they are part of the work and are necessary to proceed with high quality.

Your First Cycle: A Call to the Launchpad

We've now explored the philosophy and structure of the *Lunar Phase Framework for Success*. Any system can seem complicated from the outside, but the real understanding comes from trying it out for yourself. Just like you can't learn to swim by reading about it, you need to jump in and practice to really experience the benefits.

You don't need to master the whole system right away; you just need to take the first step. Commit to starting your first Lunar Cycle now. Choose a small, achievable goal for the next 30 days. Let this be the first step toward your bigger ambitions.

This week, try your first New Moon phase. Set aside an hour to choose one clear, modest goal for the next 30 days. It could be cleaning out the garage, cooking a few healthy meals, or writing the first ten pages of your book. Go through the process: do a quick self-audit, note your strengths, and set one or two specific, achievable goals. Write them down. Don't worry about the later phases yet, just focus on getting started. Once you begin, the next steps will follow naturally.

In the chapters ahead, we'll dive deeper into each phase of the cycle, along with practical tips to help you build the skills you need to reach your goals. You'll see how reflection leads to action, how action builds momentum, and how momentum brings renewal. This framework isn't just something to read about; it's meant to be lived and adapted to your own journey.

(4)

The New Moon

The journey begins in darkness.

We touched on this in the last chapter, but it's worth repeating: before anything visible happens, there's always a period of quiet, focused preparation. This is the New Moon: the time when the real work begins, even if no one else can see it.

In the Lunar Cycle, it's the moment the moon is invisible to us, its potential hidden as it gathers its strength for the journey ahead. In our framework, this is the phase where you become the architect of your own future. It is the most critical phase of the entire cycle, because the quality of the work you do here, in the dark, will determine the height and stability of everything you build in the light.

We tend to celebrate the visible parts of growth: the hustle, the launch, the big wins. However, we rarely discuss the quiet, behind-the-scenes work that makes those moments possible. The planning and preparation that happen out of sight are often what truly determine whether we succeed or not.

When we skip over preparation, we set ourselves up for confusion and wasted effort. Taking action without a clear plan is like spinning your wheels; you might be moving, but you're not getting anywhere. Even if you are moving fast, if you're headed in the wrong direction, you're just getting further from where you want to be. This is why the New Moon phase is important.

The New Moon phase is your chance to make sure you're headed in the right direction before you start moving. This is the time to get clear on what matters most, so your next steps actually take you where you want to go. The biggest mistake is rushing through this part, jumping into action before you've really thought everything through.

In this chapter, we'll walk through how to make the most of your New Moon phase. You'll start by taking an honest look at where you are now, then identify the unique strengths you bring to the table, and finally, pull it all together into a plan for the next cycle. This is the quiet work that will set you up for real progress as you work towards achieving your goals.

Conducting Your Life Audit

The first movement of the New Moon is an act of profound courage: the courage to look up at the sky, even though it is dark. It is far easier to live in a comfortable state of denial, telling ourselves stories about why we're not where we want to be, blaming external circumstances, and avoiding looking at the hard data of our own lives.

It's like a business that's slowly bleeding money, but the CEO refuses to look at the financial statements because they're afraid of what they'll find. That fear doesn't stop the bleeding; it just guarantees that by the time they are forced to confront the problem, it will be too late.

The first step to recovery, regardless of the problem, is to have the courage to acknowledge the unvarnished truth. You cannot change what you do not acknowledge. By having the courage to look at your life with radical honesty, you are reclaiming your power to change it. Dishonesty with yourself is the greatest transgression you can commit at this phase.

This audit isn't about criticizing yourself, but rather about taking back control. If you don't take the time to reflect on what's pulling your focus away from your true goals, you'll have a hard time getting back on track.

A powerful tool for this is a simple, daily litmus test to determine if you are happy with where you are in life. Steve Jobs famously performed an exercise each morning where he asked himself, "If today were the last day of my life, would I want to do what I am about to do today? [15]" Whenever the answer had been 'no' for too many days in a row, he knew he needed to change something.

This isn't about making drastic changes overnight. Instead, use this as a way to gather honest data about your life. For one week, start each morning by asking yourself this question. The pattern in your answers will show you where your life is out of alignment and help you see what needs your attention most.

Exercise: The Life Audit

Now it's time for a deeper, more systematic audit of the six key domains of your life. Take out a notepad and rate the following areas on a simple 1-10 scale, where 1 is a total disaster and 10 is absolutely thriving:

1. Career
2. Finances
3. Health
4. Relationships
5. Personal Growth
6. Environment

Give each area a score based on your honest, gut feeling. No one else will see this, so be truthful with yourself. Don't overthink it, just go with your first instinct.

While this is a simple exercise, you should, however, delve deeper into your questions when considering each category. For your career, don't just think about your salary; ask if your work makes you feel alive or dead inside. Does your work energize you, or does it drain every ounce of vitality from your being? Are you building skills that matter to your future, or are you treading water in a role that leads nowhere?

For your finances, don't just think about your savings; ask about the story you tell yourself about money and the anxiety it creates. Do you wake up at 3 AM worrying about bills, or do you sleep soundly knowing your financial house is in order? Are you living paycheck to paycheck, or are you building wealth that compounds over time?

For your health, consider your energy, not just the absence of illness. Do you bound out of bed in the morning ready to attack the day, or do you drag yourself through each hour fueled by caffeine and willpower alone? Can you play with your children without getting winded, or climb a flight of stairs without your heart pounding?

For relationships, assess if they are a source of strength or a source of drain. Do the people closest to you lift you up and challenge you to become better, or do they pull you down into negativity and mediocrity? Are your relationships built on mutual respect and genuine connection, or are they transactional obligations that leave you feeling empty?

For your environment, ask if your physical space is a sanctuary for your best self or a chaotic reflection of a cluttered mind. Does your home inspire creativity and peace, or does it add to your daily stress? Is your workspace conducive to deep focus and productivity, or is it a constant source of distraction and frustration?

Once you've scored each area, you'll see where your biggest opportunities for growth are. Focus on the lowest scores first. Ask yourself not just what needs to change, but why. When you get to the root of the problem, you'll know what to let go of so you can make room for what matters.

The Art of Intentional Pruning

This is where we begin to borrow a term from arborists called **Intentional Pruning**. Before you can add new missions to your life, you must first make space for them. Just as you need to trim a tree to ensure it grows in a desirable direction, you have to trim areas of your life that are keeping you from achieving the goals you desire.

We often cling to jobs or projects that are no longer serving us because of the sunk cost fallacy: the idea that we've already invested so much time and energy that it feels like a waste to abandon the effort. The problem with this reasoning, however, is that no matter what you do, you can't recoup the time, energy, and money you've already invested in the effort; instead, you simply keep digging even deeper in the wrong direction by continuing down that path.

With this being said, the New Moon phase is about looking forward, not backward. Instead of focusing on what you've already spent, focus on your future potential. Remember, the darkness now is just the beginning of a brighter phase ahead.

To decide which areas to prune or nurture, take a close look at your audit scores. For the true disasters, the "1s" and "2s," the answer is often to prune some of the items in these areas from your life completely if at all possible. These are the energy drainers, the toxic relationships, the soul-crushing obligations that provide no value and extract everything from you.

For the things that are working well, the "8s" and "9s," the strategy is to nurture and protect them. These are your sources of strength, the areas where you're already aligned with your *Orbiting Ambition*, and you must defend them against the encroachment of lesser priorities.

For everything in the middle, the answer is likely to restructure. You may not need to prune the entire branch, but perhaps you can change the terms of your engagement. You may be able to renegotiate your role or set new boundaries at work. You may be able to shift focus onto a different project or change the type of work you're doing for the company. You may make changes to your living situation or move to a different town or city that better fits your needs. This process of intentional pruning and restructuring is essential; it involves clearing away dead branches so that new, vibrant growth can emerge.

Once you've determined what to prune, you must then turn your attention to the complex knot of problems, anxieties, and ambitions that remain. Think of this as the central challenge of your New Moon phase: learning the art of untangling the knot.

Untangling the Knot: Finding Root Causes

Just like everything else in life, problems are rarely simple and straightforward. In most cases, they're a tangle of threads. The surface-level symptom, such as feeling constantly tired or unhappy, is just the most visible loop. Your first task is to isolate a single thread and begin to follow it. This is the essence of untangling your knot. Each time you ask "why?", you are patiently following that one thread deeper into the tangle, loosening the knot as you go, until you arrive at the very beginning: the original twist that created the problem.

For example, "I'm always tired" may be the visible loop, but by untangling it, you might find a core thread of deep financial anxiety that keeps you awake at night, which stems from a pattern of overspending to fill an emotional void, which itself comes from a childhood belief that you're only valuable when you're successful in the eyes of others.

Often, what you find at the start of the thread is not just a tactical problem, but a deep, underlying story you've been telling yourself for years. These are your **limiting beliefs**, and they are the oldest, tightest threads in the knot. They are the invisible pieces that hold the entire tangle in place. The first step to reclaiming your power is to see these beliefs not as facts, but as the original threads they are. Coupled with this should be the realization that any thread can be pulled loose.

To do this, you must first identify the recurring narrative of negativity in your head. What are you telling yourself that you can't do? What do you think you're bad at? What do you believe about yourself that is "unfixable?" These recurring negative narratives are most often large stereotypes that you've placed on yourself due to a negative experience in the past.

Once you've identified the recurring narrative, follow that thread back to its origin. Where did you first learn that you are incapable of solving this problem? Did you have a bad experience in school that made you think you are bad at writing or math? Did you have a vehicle collision that makes you believe you are a bad driver? Did you have a failed business venture that makes you think you are bad at business? Did a parent or teacher tell you that you weren't talented enough, smart enough, or disciplined enough?

This isn't about doubting yourself; it's about understanding where your limiting beliefs come from. When you view them as old stories, rather than current reality, you can begin to let them go.

Now comes the most important part: start searching for evidence that challenges your old story. It's time to play defense attorney for your own potential; you're up against a dirty prosecutor who is making up evidence against you. Hunt for every moment that disproves the limiting belief, even if those moments feel insignificant.

Maybe you think you're "bad with money." Okay, look for the times you made a smart financial move, no matter how small. Did you shop around before making a big purchase? Did you walk away from an impulse buy? Did you save up for something special instead of running up your credit card? These moments are real, even if your brain is used to ignoring them. Write them down. Build your own case for the defense; you're not on trial, but your old story is.

Now you can start to replace those old beliefs with new, stronger ones. Instead of thinking, "I'm bad with money," you might say, "I'm learning to make better financial choices."

Notice the shift: "I am learning." This reminds you that growth is a process, and you don't have to be perfect right away. As you change these core beliefs, the knot starts to loosen, and new possibilities begin to appear.

As the knot loosens, you may start to notice something remarkable: not all the threads are a problem. Woven into the mess are fibers that are incredibly strong, uniquely textured, and full of potential. These are your advantages, your superpowers, waiting to be recognized and deployed.

Your job is not just to untangle the bad, but to identify and reclaim the good. Some of your greatest advantages are the threads forged in your greatest struggles; they are thicker and have more grip precisely because they've been tested. Your past struggles are not liabilities; they are the strongest fibers in your possession.

But often, these powerful threads are hidden in plain sight, buried within the knot. To find them, you must intentionally search for them. One method that is incredibly powerful for this is what I call the Thread Inventory.

Exercise: The Thread Inventory

The premise is simple: set a timer for 10 minutes and force yourself to list at least 30 unique facts, skills, or experiences from your entire life. The goal of this exercise is to bypass your curated, professional self.

The first 10 facts will come easily; they are the polished threads of your résumé (things such as "successfully managed a team for a high-visibility project," or "graduated with honors"). The next 10 will be harder, forcing you to dig into past jobs, hobbies, and travels.

The real magic is what happens in the final 10. When your brain is tired and feels empty, it will start to offer up the strange, forgotten, and seemingly irrelevant threads.

List the summer you went to camp and learned basic survival skills. List the blue ribbon you won for a science fair project in seventh grade. List the fact that you taught yourself how to write HTML so that you could create your own website. List the childhood obsession you had with learning about stage lighting and special effects. List the time you organized a neighborhood yard sale and negotiated with twenty different families. List the semester you spent abroad and had to navigate a foreign city with a language you barely spoke. Do not judge these threads. Just get them on the page.

When the timer is done, review the final list. Buried in there is the raw material of your unique genius. The summer at camp taught you about grit and the importance of preparation. The science fair project was your first taste of obsessive research, and winning the blue ribbon gave you the confidence to pursue other projects. Learning HTML was an early sign of a love for building systems. The obsession with stage lighting was a foundation of your love for learning how things work. The yard sale demonstrated early negotiation and project management skills. The semester abroad proved that you could adapt and thrive in uncertain situations.

These aren't just facts; they're the building blocks of your character and skills. They show you what you're capable of, even if you've forgotten. You've been building your own Constellation of Skills throughout your entire life, often without noticing.

The Personal Mission Briefing

Once you complete your Life Audit and have this rich inventory of your foundational threads, it's time to organize your findings into a coherent strategy. This isn't just about knowing yourself; it's about preparing yourself for the journey ahead. To do this, we will conduct a Personal Mission Briefing, a framework adapted from the classic SWOT analysis, designed to give you a clear, honest picture of your inner and outer landscape. Think of this as the final intelligence report you review before launching your first Lunar Cycle.

Grab a piece of paper and create four quadrants on the page. Label one quadrant for each of the following areas:

1. Strengths (Top-Left Quadrant)

Here, list your strongest internal assets. Look back at your Thread Inventory and the areas where you scored highest in your Life Audit. What patterns do you see? Your strengths aren't just what's on your résumé; they're the core threads that run through your life.

Are you a natural system builder who instinctively knows how to create order? Are you the "calm in the chaos," the person everyone turns to in a crisis because you can think clearly when others panic? Are you a relentless researcher, someone who can dive into any topic and emerge with a deep understanding? Are you a connector, someone who naturally builds bridges between people and ideas?

Write down the 3-5 strengths that feel most true to you. These are the engines that drive your ambition: both the natural talents you were born with and the skills you've refined over time.

2. Weaknesses (Top-Right Quadrant)

This part takes real honesty. A weakness isn't a flaw; it's just a thread that needs attention. Review your lowest scores and the limiting beliefs you identified earlier.

Do you have a deep-seated fear of public speaking that prevents you from sharing your ideas? Do you have a tendency to procrastinate on financial matters, letting bills pile up until they become crises? Do you lack technical skills in a critical area that's holding back your business idea? Are you conflict-averse, avoiding difficult conversations that need to happen? Are you a chronic perfectionist who struggles to ship work because it's never quite good enough?

Listing your weaknesses isn't about criticizing yourself; it's about seeing where you need support or growth. It can also show you where to look for help from others whose strengths balance out your own.

3. Opportunities (Bottom-Left Quadrant)

Opportunities are external factors in the world that are aligned with your strengths. Given your unique strengths, what trends, technologies, or unmet needs can you see on the horizon?

If your strength lies in building systems and you notice small businesses struggling with inefficiency, that's an opportunity. If your strength is empathetic communication and you sense a world growing lonelier by the day, that's an opportunity. If your strength is visual storytelling and you see brands desperate for content they can't afford to produce, that's an opportunity.

This quadrant is where your unique capability intersects with unmet need. Note, these don't have to be detailed and specific; they can be vague opportunities that you see as possibilities you can capitalize   on.

4. Threats (Bottom-Right Quadrant)

Threats are external factors that could exploit your weaknesses or derail your mission. What is happening in the world, your industry, or your personal life that could pose a challenge?

Are there rising costs or economic pressures that threaten your financial stability? Is there a market shift that could make your current path obsolete? Are there personal commitments or family obligations that will demand your time and energy during your mission? Are there health concerns that could limit your capacity? Are there emerging competitors who are better funded or more experienced?

Recognizing threats isn't being negative, it's being prepared. It's the difference between being caught off guard and having a plan in place.

**orbiting
ambition**

Strengths	Weaknesses
Opportunities	Threats

Figure 2: SWOT Analysis Format Example

Figure 2 above illustrates the overall structure of your SWOT Analysis. Once you've filled out all four quadrants, you have your Mission Briefing. This one-page document provides a clear map for your entire journey. Your strengths and opportunities indicate where to focus your energy, while your weaknesses and threats highlight areas that require your attention.

This framework doesn't just provide a list of qualities; it offers a dynamic map of reality. It shows you the terrain you're about to traverse, the resources you're bringing to the journey, and the obstacles you'll need to navigate around. It is from this map that you can now begin to plot a truly intelligent course by setting goals that leverage your power, mitigate your risks, and move you confidently into your first orbit.

Defining Your Liberation Goal

Now that you've finished your Life Audit, Thread Inventory, and Mission Briefing, it's time to bring it all together. The next step is to set a goal that helps you use your strengths and opportunities, while working to overcome your weaknesses and threats. I call this your **Liberation Goal**.

Positive goals are important, but a Liberation Goal goes a step further. It names not just what you want to achieve, but what you want to **break free** from. This works because we're often more motivated to escape pain than to chase a vague idea of success. The fear of staying stuck can be a powerful push to move forward.

"I want to be financially secure" is a nice goal; however, "I am breaking free from the humiliation of having my card declined at the grocery store" is a visceral, motivating mission. It provides a different kind of fuel: the kind that burns hot when your motivation wanes and you need to remember why you started.

To begin ideating your Liberation Goal, examine the root problems identified in your audit, particularly those that scored 1, 2, or 3. Your Liberation Goal for this cycle should be a clear, defiant statement of the freedom you will achieve by completing this goal. Let me give you some examples to illustrate the difference:

Goal: "I want to improve my physical fitness."

Liberation Goal: "I am breaking free from the shame of avoiding mirrors and the fear of health problems that could steal my best years."

Goal: "I want to advance my career."

Liberation Goal: "I am liberating myself from the suffocating feeling of being overlooked and undervalued, of watching less qualified people get promoted while I stay invisible."

Can you feel the difference? Goals are good, but Liberation Goals have real energy. They give you something specific to fight against. When things get tough, remembering what you're breaking free from can give you the fuel to keep going.

Write your Liberation Goal now. Be specific and honest about what you want to escape. This isn't about being negative; it's about using your dissatisfaction to fuel positive change. Your Liberation

Goal pulls you away from what you don't want, while your SMART goals pull you toward what you do want. Together, they create a powerful push and pull that will ultimately help you achieve your *Orbiting Ambition*.

Crafting Your SMART Goals

By now, you've defined your *Orbiting Ambition*, looked honestly at your strengths and weaknesses, and set a Liberation Goal to break free from what's holding you back. Now it's time to set the positive goals you want to achieve in this cycle.

If you've studied business, you'll be familiar with the concept of SMART goals, which is setting goals that are Specific, Measurable, Attainable, Relevant, and Time-Bound.[16] It is critical that the goals you set meet these criteria, because you'll want to be able to specify with pinpoint accuracy when you have completed the goal, so that you can move on to the next part of the process.

Making your goals SMART helps you stay accountable. When your goals are specific, measurable, achievable, relevant, and time-bound, you can clearly track your progress. Reaching these goals, cycle after cycle, is what will move you closer to your *Orbiting Ambition*.

Let's break down each element of SMART goals in detail:

Specific: Your goal must be crystal clear, leaving no room for ambiguity. A vague goal, such as "I want to be healthier," provides no direction. A specific goal, such as "I will walk 10,000 steps per day, five days per week," tells you exactly what success looks like. The test of specificity is simple: could someone else read your goal and know exactly what you need to do? If there's any confusion about what "counts" as achieving the goal, it's not specific enough.

Measurable: You must be able to quantify your progress. This is what transforms a wish into a goal. "I want to write a book" is not a measurable goal. "I will write 500 words per day" is measurable, as it is possible to count the words. The beauty of measurable goals is that they give you real-time feedback. You know, at any given moment, whether you're on track or falling behind. This removes the ambiguity and the ability to lie to yourself about your progress.

Attainable: This is where you must strike a balance between ambition and reality. Your goal should stretch you, but not break you. If you haven't exercised in five years, setting a goal to run a marathon next month is not attainable; in fact, it's delusional, and it sets you up for failure and injury. But setting a goal to run a 5K in three months might be perfectly attainable with consistent training. The key is to look at your current situation honestly and set goals that are just beyond your current capacity, but within reach if you commit to the work. As you complete cycles and build your capabilities, your definition of "attainable" will expand dramatically.

Relevant: Your goal must be aligned with your *Orbiting Ambition* and your Liberation Goal. This is the filter that keeps you from chasing shiny objects. Just because a goal is achievable doesn't mean it's worth achieving. If your *Orbiting Ambition* is to build financial freedom so you can spend more time with your family, then a goal that requires you to work 80-hour weeks for the next year may not be relevant, as it could be actively working against your true mission. Every goal you set should, upon completion, move you measurably closer to your *Orbiting Ambition*. If it doesn't, it's a distraction.

Time-Bound: Every goal needs a deadline. Without a deadline, a goal is just a wish. The deadline creates urgency, it prevents procrastination, and it allows you to assess your progress. "I will write a book someday" has no power. "I will complete the first draft of my book by June 1st" creates a forcing function. The Lunar Cycle framework naturally provides this time-bound structure, as you work in 30-, 60-, or 90-day sprints. Furthermore, within each cycle, you will have weekly and even daily time-bound process goals that keep you on track.

Take some time to choose the first few goals you want to work on. Choose no more than three, so you don't lose focus. For each one, decide how you'll measure success and set a clear deadline. Then, prioritize your goals and make a simple plan for your next steps.

Let's make this practical. Suppose your *Orbiting Ambition* is to build genuine financial independence, and your Liberation Goal is to break free from the constant weight of financial insecurity. You're tired of the cycle of just getting by, and exhausted by the quiet fear that one unexpected expense could undo your progress. Here's a 90-day Lunar Cycle that could help you get started:

Goal 1 (Outcome): Build and launch a small-scale income stream that generates at least $500 per month by Day 90.

- **Specific**: One defined side income source such as freelance work, a digital product, or an online service.
- **Measurable**: $500 monthly target by end of cycle.

- **Attainable**: Modest enough to be achievable within 90 days.
- **Relevant**: Moves directly toward financial freedom and confidence.
- **Time-Bound**: 90-day window for creation, launch, and validation.

Goal 2 (Process): Dedicate two focused hours every evening, Monday through Friday, to building, marketing, or refining this income stream.

- **Specific**: Consistent schedule and focused task window.
- **Measurable**: Hours logged and milestones completed.
- **Attainable**: Sustainable commitment alongside existing responsibilities.
- **Relevant**: Converts intention into tangible momentum.
- **Time-Bound**: 90-day duration, five sessions per week.

Goal 3 (Skill-Building): Read one high-impact personal finance book within the next 45 days, and apply at least three key principles to your budgeting or income plan.

- **Specific**: One chosen book, three applied takeaways.
- **Measurable**: Completion of the book and implemented strategies.
- **Attainable**: Manageable pace of a few chapters per week.
- **Relevant**: Strengthens financial habits and mindset.
- **Time-Bound**: 45-day reading and application window.

Together, these goals work as a system: the outcome gives you security, the process builds momentum, and the skill gives you wisdom. You're not just earning extra money, you're building the confidence and habits that make financial freedom possible.

Overcoming Your Planning Biases

Before you finalize your blueprint, it is also important that you confront the hidden biases that sabotage even the most well-intentioned plans. Your brain, for all its brilliance, has some predictable bugs in its operating system. Understanding these bugs and designing around them is what separates successful plans from fantasy.

The first is the **Planning Fallacy**, a term coined by Nobel laureates Daniel Kahneman and Amos Tversky. It is our natural tendency to vastly underestimate the time, cost, and risks of future actions, while overestimating their benefits.[17] It's the reason why every home renovation project seems to take twice as long and cost twice as much as the initial "realistic" estimate. We are pathologically optimistic when we are in the safe, comfortable armchair of the planning phase. We imagine a perfect world where nothing goes wrong, where we're always motivated, and where unexpected obstacles never arise. This isn't just naïve, it's dangerous.

This is often combined with **Overconfidence Bias**, which I call the "Couch to 5K" Syndrome. When you're creating your plan, you are imagining a superhero version of yourself who is always motivated, always disciplined, never gets sick, never has family emergencies, and never faces unexpected work demands. The person who hasn't worked out in five years creates a detailed plan to hit the gym six days a week for 90 minutes. This plan isn't for them; it's for a fictional character. When their real, human self inevitably fails to live up to this impossible standard, they don't blame the plan. Instead, they blame themselves and choose to abandon the entire mission.

To counteract these biases, you need to plan with **realistic optimism**, the balance between belief and preparation.[18] Most people dramatically underestimate the time it takes to complete meaningful work, and they become discouraged when it takes longer than expected. It's not because they're lazy or naïve; it's because they forget that life has gravity. You always encounter unexpected roadblocks that may cause the length or cost of your endeavor to increase.

A better approach is to plan for resistance. Take your best guess at how long something will take, then double it. Not because you expect to fail, but because you're making space for real life. If you think you can finish something in a week, give yourself two. If you plan for a month, allow for two months.

The goal isn't to slow progress; it's to ensure completion and to keep you from abandoning the project due to slow growth. If you happen to exceed your goal and finish early, great. If you encounter roadblocks that require it to take longer, there's still no harm, no foul.

This isn't pessimism. It's realism and respect for the friction, anticipation of the unexpected, and realization of the truth that meaningful work always takes longer than we wish, but never longer than it's worth.

After you've defined the scope of your mission for the cycle, take a breath and cut it in half. If your goal was to write four chapters of your book, change it to two. If it were to lose 20 pounds, change it to 10. If it were to acquire 50 new clients, change it to 25.

I'm sure this feels wrong after you've set a SMART goal, and your ambitious mind is likely screaming that you're selling yourself short. However, here's the truth: the goal of your first few cycles is not to achieve a monumental outcome; it is to establish the habit of success and generate momentum.

You will achieve far more in the long run by successfully completing a series of modest, realistic goals than you will by repeatedly failing at overly ambitious ones. Success breeds confidence, which in turn breeds even more success. Failure breeds doubt, which breeds more failure. Start with wins you can achieve, and let your ambition grow with your capabilities.

The Inversion Method

Now for one final, powerful technique to make your plan truly resilient. It's a mental model famously used by Charlie Munger called **inversion**. James Clear discusses this idea thoroughly in an article, and the concept is to think about your goal in reverse so that you can anticipate mistakes that could lead to failure.[19]

When we design our goals, we typically think about the best-case scenario. We think about what it takes to win, how we're going to beat the odds, and why this time will be the successful attempt. This optimism is great, and it is a crucial component of planning for success; however, it is also easy to get caught up in the best-case scenario and overlook preventable mistakes ahead of time. For this exercise, instead of asking, "What do I need to do to succeed?" you invert the question and ask, "What could I do to guarantee that I fail?"

This exercise helps you see your plan from a new angle. Instead of just imagining success, you look honestly at what could go wrong. This way, you can spot risks and weak spots you might have missed.

Here's how to do it: Take your beautifully crafted goal and all of the work you've done thus far to plan the cycle. Now, fast-forward in your mind to the end of the cycle. Instead of seeing an end where you completed your goal, imagine that it has been a complete and utter disaster. You have failed spectacularly. Your goal is not just unmet, but it's catastrophically off the mark.

Now, spend a few minutes thinking about the story of why you failed. What happened? What specific actions did you take, or fail to take, that led to this outcome? What unexpected obstacles arose that you weren't prepared for? What personal weaknesses of yours got in the way? What assumptions did you make that turned out to be completely wrong?

Did you underestimate the amount of time the project would take? Did you overestimate your own discipline? Did you fail to communicate your plans to someone important in your life, causing conflict? Did you neglect your health and burn out halfway through? Did you get distracted by a shiny new opportunity? Did you let perfectionism prevent you from shipping work? Did you fail to ask for help when you needed it?

Write out your failure story in detail. Make it real. By imagining all the ways things could go wrong, you can spot the pitfalls ahead of time. This is your chance to test your plan before you start.

Once you have considered your failure scenario, review it and highlight the biggest, most likely points of failure. For each one, ask yourself: "Can I adjust my cycle plan right now to prevent or mitigate this risk?"

Perhaps you've realized that your biggest risk is overcommitting your time, so you build in buffer weeks to your schedule. Maybe you see that you'll need childcare support during your writing time, so you have that conversation with your partner now instead of hoping it works out. Perhaps you recognize that you lack an accountability mechanism, so you commit to a weekly check-in with a friend or mentor. Maybe you realize you're planning to do everything yourself when you should be delegating or outsourcing certain tasks.

This is how you take your plan from a hopeful idea to something that can actually stand up to the real world. By stress-testing your blueprint before you ever take action, you shore up the weak spots and make your strategy resilient.

Inversion isn't just a clever trick; it's your edge. It's how you approach your life like a CEO, anticipating what could go wrong and making sure you're ready for it. You're not just planning for victory; you're making your plan tough enough to survive the fight.

Assembling Your One-Page Mission Roadmap

Now it's time to bring everything together into one simple page: your One-Page Mission Roadmap. This isn't a long plan you'll forget about; it's a living document you'll use to stay on track.

Your One-Page Mission Roadmap should include the following:

1. **Your *Orbiting Ambition*** (1-2 sentences at the top): This is your North Star. Every goal on this page should be in service of this larger purpose.
2. **Your Mission for This Cycle** (1 sentence): What is the specific, overarching achievement you're going after in the next 30, 60, or 90 days?
3. **Your Liberation Goal** (1 sentence): What pain are you breaking free from? What cage are you escaping?
4. **Your SMART Goals** (3 goals maximum): One goal for the outcome of this cycle, one goal for process improvement, and one goal for skill-building.
5. **Your Unfair Advantages** (2-3 bullet points): What are your top 1-3 strengths that you'll leverage to achieve this mission?
6. **Your Known Risks & Mitigation Plans** (3-5 bullet points): From your Inversion exercise, what are the top ways this could fail, and what's your plan to prevent each one?
7. **Your Weekly Milestones** (4-12 milestones depending on cycle length): Break your 90-day mission into weekly checkpoints. What does progress look like each week?

This one page is your compass. Print it out and place it somewhere you'll see every day, such as on your mirror, desk, or fridge. Use it daily to stay focused on your mission.

The Ignition Test: Does Your Plan Have Fire?

Before you finish your New Moon phase and start taking action, there's one last test: the **Ignition Test**. Read your mission, your Liberation Goal, and your SMART goals out loud. Go through your whole Mission Roadmap from top to bottom.

Now, pay attention to your body. Does it have ignition? Do you feel a spark, a sense of authentic excitement and forward momentum rising in your chest? Does your heart rate quicken slightly? Do you feel that electric anticipation of beginning something meaningful? Or does it feel heavy, like a pile of joyless obligations, or like homework?

This feeling is very important. If your plan feels heavy, dead, or obligatory, then something is wrong. Your plan isn't aligned with your authentic goals, and it's not connected to your true *Orbiting Ambition*. This is a sign that you've been infected by someone else's expectations, by Linear Ambition, or by a "should" that isn't genuinely yours.

Go back to your *Orbiting Ambition* and ask yourself the three questions again: What makes you forget to eat? What makes you righteously pissed off? What do you want to be known for? Ensure your mission for this cycle is a genuine expression of your deeper purpose. Adjust your goals until the Ignition Test passes, until reading your roadmap fills you with that sense of energized excitement that drives you forward.

The work of the New Moon is not complete until you feel this fire. This is because the fire is what will sustain you through the difficult middle of the Waxing Phases, when motivation fades and discipline must carry you forward. If the plan doesn't light you up in the quiet of the New Moon, it will never sustain you in the chaos of execution.

(5)

Building Your Constellation of Skills

By now, you've learned how to move through your own New Moon. You've seen how to pause, reflect, and get honest about where you are and what you want. You've started to find your own guiding light in the darkness, and you've begun to map out your next steps before jumping into action. But there's something easy to overlook: the New Moon isn't just a time for planning. It's also the perfect moment to intentionally build the skills and strengths that will make your next cycle of growth even more powerful than the last.

Each time you complete a cycle, your real progress isn't measured by how many boxes you checked off, but by how much you've grown. The goal isn't to pile on more tasks or keep yourself endlessly busy. Instead, it's about focusing on the skills and strengths that matter most for your journey. There's a big difference between staying busy and making real progress. True growth happens when you move beyond "just doing" and start building momentum that actually lifts you higher.

Many people attempt to develop skills in a scattered manner; they pick up whatever seems interesting or useful in the moment, or simply learn as they go. Curiosity is great, but without a sense of direction, it's easy to end up wandering, like walking through a forest without a map. To make real progress, you need to be intentional about which skills you choose to develop and understand why they matter for your path.

The *Lunar Phase Framework* gives you a natural rhythm for taking action. In this chapter, we'll look at how to choose and develop skills in a way that builds on itself, so each cycle of growth becomes more valuable than the last. This is how you move from just checking off goals to becoming someone who is ready for bigger challenges and greater achievements, one cycle at a time.

Skill-Building: The Secret to Value Multiplication

When I started my DJ business at the age of thirteen, I had one profitable skill: I could play music and bring stage lights to parties to entertain a crowd. While this was a valuable skill to possess, it had a ceiling on its own. I could improve at reading crowds, building playlists, and managing equipment, but fundamentally, I was trading time for money. One event, one payment. Two events, two payments. The math was linear.

A couple of years later, I learned how to write code and started to master the craft of website design. Suddenly, I had two skills that I could offer to clients, even though they were vastly different in nature. However, what I didn't realize at the time was that two skills aren't just additive. When chosen strategically, skills complement and enhance each other's value, multiplying your total overall value.

Website design didn't just enable me to build websites for clients; it also allowed me to market my DJ business more effectively, showcase my work professionally, and ultimately led to corporate clients hiring me for multiple services. I then learned about online marketing, radio advertising, and aerial video production, all of which multiplied my capabilities even further. The combination was worth more than the sum of its parts.

This is the principle of **skill stacking**, and understanding it is the difference between building a career through accumulation versus building one through multiplication. When you stack complementary skills, each new capability doesn't just add to your value; it amplifies everything you already know how to do.[20]

Think about the most valuable people in any organization. They're rarely the ones who are world-class at just one thing. They're the people who combine three or four high-level capabilities in unique ways. The engineer who can also communicate complex ideas clearly and simplistically. The salesperson who understands the technical product deeply. The creative who understands business strategy. The analyst who can tell compelling stories with data.

So, the real question is: which skills should you focus on, and in what order, to create the most powerful combinations for your own journey?

This is where many people get off track, as they become entranced chasing whatever is popular or seems impressive, without considering how it fits with their own strengths. The right skills for you are the ones that build on what you already have and move you closer to your own ambitions. Your approach to skill-building should be personal, thoughtful, and aligned with the direction you want to go. This is why the first step is to realize the skills you currently have and think about what new skills could complement them best.

The Skill Orbit: Understanding Your Constellation

Imagine your skills as stars orbiting around the center of your ambition. Not every skill holds the same weight, and not all are worth the same investment of your time and energy. The first step is to understand how your unique Constellation of Skills is arranged, so you can build it with intention.

Closest to the center are your core skills: the few abilities that define your craft and identity. These are the engines that power your orbit: writing, coding, teaching, designing, leading, selling, analyzing. Without these foundational capabilities, you drift aimlessly. These are the skills you cannot outsource, the ones that make you who you are in your field. If these deteriorate, your entire orbit collapses.

Beyond your core skills are your auxiliary skills: supportive capabilities that amplify your reach without replacing your core strengths. A great designer who learns storytelling doesn't stop being a designer; they become a designer who can articulate value and persuade stakeholders. A skilled engineer who learns persuasion doesn't abandon technical work; they become someone who can lead projects and influence decisions. These outer-orbit skills often determine the scale of your impact, the difference between being competent and being irreplaceable.

But here's the challenge: every skill you add takes time and energy to keep sharp. If you try to collect too many, you end up spreading yourself thin, and nothing gets the attention it needs to really grow. The key is to find balance and build a Constellation of Skills that work together and support your core strengths.

To find that balance, ask yourself three grounding questions during your New Moon planning:

1. **Which skills sustain my craft?**

   These are non-negotiable. They're what you're known for, what clients pay you for, what makes you valuable in the first place. Neglect these, and your orbit decays.

2. **Which skills expand my influence or efficiency?**

   These are strategic investments. They don't replace what you do; they multiply how effectively you can do it or how far your impact can reach.

3. **Which skills drain energy without creating value?**

These are the "black holes" of your constellation. They look impressive on paper, but they consume resources without producing meaningful returns. If a skill doesn't serve the first two categories, it belongs in someone else's Constellation of Skills, not yours.

Many people have difficulty building a true Constellation of Skills, which leads to them being "pigeonholed" in their careers. They don't get stuck due to a lack of motivation, but because they focus too narrowly on just one area. They become experts in a single skill but struggle to apply it to new opportunities or different fields.

Real growth happens when you start to build bridges between your skills. When you combine communication with expertise, creativity with action, or technical knowledge with big-picture thinking, you open up new possibilities. These intersections are where your future opportunities will come from, and they will be the magic glue that holds together your Constellation of Skills and makes you marketable.

The Skill Intersection: Where Your Skills Meet Needs

Building your skills isn't about trying to master everything. It's about discovering where your natural strengths meet real needs in the world. The goal is to find a shared space where your abilities open up new opportunities. To do this, you can create a simple Venn Diagram to help you determine where your skills intersect.

In your Venn Diagram, one circle represents your Core Strengths. These are the things you do very well, and are the types of skills that feel like extensions of who you are, rather than obligations you force yourself through. These are your gravitational constants: your natural communication ability, your analytical mind, your creative intuition, your capacity to teach, to organize, to empathize, to lead. These are the capabilities that energize you rather than deplete you, and is the work that makes you forget to eat.

The other circle represents Market Demand, which are the external forces shaping opportunities in your industry, community, and field. These are the problems people are willing to pay to solve, the inefficiencies begging for innovation, the human needs that still lack clarity, comfort, or connection. This isn't about chasing trends; it's about recognizing genuine, persistent needs that aren't being adequately met.

Where these two circles overlap is your Skill Intersection: the place where your personal strengths meet what the world actually needs. This is where you should focus your next steps. Instead of learning at random, you're choosing skills that truly matter for your journey and your goals. See **Figure 3** on the next page for an illustration of this diagram.

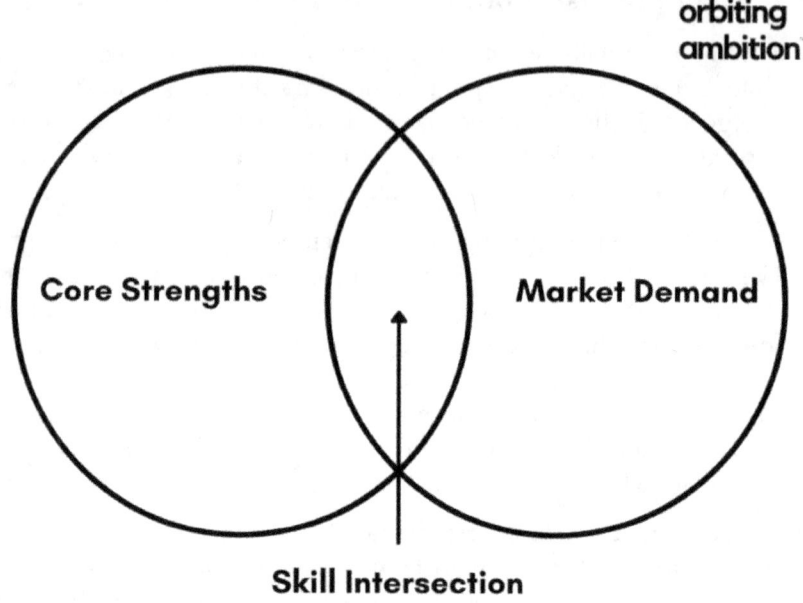

Skill Intersection

Figure 3: Skill Intersection

Let me give you concrete examples of what this looks like in practice:

If your strength is organization and systems thinking, and you see small businesses drowning in operational chaos with scattered tools and inefficient workflows, the Skill Intersection might be learning automation tools or workflow design. You're not abandoning your organizational strength; you're multiplying it through technology.

If your strength is visual creativity and design, and you observe that content dominates every platform but most of it is forgettable and poorly executed, the Skill Intersection might be learning branding strategy or digital storytelling. You're not becoming less of a designer; you're becoming a designer who understands why design matters and how to make it strategic.

If your strength is analytical thinking and problem-solving, and you notice that teams are drowning in data but starving for insight, the Skill Intersection might be learning data visualization or communication. You're not diluting your analytical capabilities; you're making them accessible and actionable for others.

If your strength is empathy and understanding people, and you see workplaces craving authenticity and struggling with culture, the Skill Intersection might be learning coaching frameworks or facilitation techniques. You're not replacing empathy with methodology; you're giving your natural gift a professional structure that creates measurable impact.

Each of these examples illustrates the same truth: your growth accelerates when you develop skills at the intersection of your unique strengths and real needs around you. That shared space isn't just luck; it's the natural pull that brings new opportunities your way. As the rapper Pitbull famously said, "The harder I work, the luckier I get."[21] The key is to develop skills that enable you to capitalize on the opportunities that come your way.

Here's where most people go off track: they either build skills just because they're interested in a particular subject (and ignore what the world actually needs), or they chase whatever is popular (and ignore their own strengths). The first path makes you good at things no one values. The second path makes you average at things everyone else is already doing. Neither one gives you the leverage you need.

The Skill Intersection reminds you that learning is not about accumulation; it's about connection. Every new capability should link to the gravitational center of your *Orbiting Ambition* and pull something larger into orbit. Over time, these overlaps form a true constellation: a system of interconnected strengths that reinforce one another and extend your reach in ways that isolated skills never could.

Intentional Skill Tracking and Development

As you move through your Lunar Cycles, it's easy to keep pushing forward without noticing the skills you've picked up along the way. However, tracking your skills as you grow each cycle is incredibly useful, as it helps you make the most of your new abilities in future cycles.

To help with this, you can use something as simple as a notepad to track your skills as you move through the planning, action, and review parts of each cycle. To add structure to this, however, here are three systems you can use to track your skills as you move through the Lunar Cycle:

1. The Capture System

Create a dedicated place to record insights and lessons as they occur. This can be a single document, app, or notebook where knowledge accumulates instead of evaporating. The key is consistency of location. Don't scatter insights across random sticky notes, text messages to yourself, and half-remembered thoughts. Centralize them.

When you read something valuable, capture it immediately. When you apply a new technique and it works, document it. When you make a mistake, record what you learned.

Learning compounds only when it's revisited. A scattered collection of insights is worthless. A centralized, searchable repository becomes an asset that grows in value with every addition.

2. The Practice System

Schedule fixed blocks of time for skill development each week that are non-negotiable windows protected from distraction, treated with the same seriousness you'd give a client meeting or a doctor's appointment. Even an hour per week, repeated consistently across a year, becomes transformative. That's 52 hours of focused practice, which is sufficient to transition from a complete novice to functional competence in most skills.

The block doesn't have to be long. What matters is that it is consistent and protected. No emails, no meetings, no multitasking.

This is your time for deliberate practice, and it is a commitment you make to your future self.

3. The Review System

At the end of each Lunar Cycle, you'll be in the Waning Phases, where you'll recover and review your cycle's progress. Here, you can also assess what you learned and how it improved your orbit. Ask what worked, what didn't, and what you'll refine next time. This keeps progress visible and ensures no cycle repeats aimlessly.

Without review, you might finish cycles without learning anything from them. You'll stay busy, but you won't be moving forward. The review system forces you to pause and ask yourself: Am I actually getting better, or am I just repeating the same level over and over?

That's the difference between experience and expertise. Experience is just time passing. Expertise is what happens when you reflect on your experience and actually integrate what you've learned.

When you have these three systems — Capture, Practice, and Review — in place, growth starts to sustain itself. You're no longer relying on motivation or willpower alone. Instead, you're relying on a structure that works for you, even on days when you don't feel inspired.

The Rhythm of Progress

Like most things, skill mastery isn't a straight line. You don't just learn something once and move on. You come back to it from a higher level each time, seeing new details you missed before and applying it in ways you couldn't have imagined when you first started.

The skills that helped you this year will keep evolving next year. What once took all your focus becomes second nature, running in the background while you take on new challenges. What was once hard becomes instinct: something you do without even thinking about it.

In each Lunar Cycle, you're not just learning new things, you're building a rhythm of progress. It's like a good workout routine: keeping up the rhythm and staying consistent is how you get stronger and grow. You're teaching yourself how to keep moving, even as your ambitions shift, your goals change, and new possibilities come into view.

That's what separates people who burn out from those who keep rising year after year. The first group relies on inspiration; they work when they feel motivated and slow down when they don't. The second group relies on rhythm. They've built systems and cycles that keep them moving forward, no matter how they feel or what's happening around them.

Inspiration is a spark. Rhythm is a steady fire that keeps you going through every season. While inspiration is helpful, it's rhythm that lets you grow, cycle after cycle.

⑥

The Waxing Phases

By now, you have taken the time to clarify your vision, align it with your true motivations, and start building the skills you need to move forward. You are no longer just imagining what could be; you are preparing yourself to take real action.

With your plan in hand, you're ready to move from intention to action. These are the Waxing Phases: the part of the Lunar Cycle when the moon starts to reveal itself, growing brighter each night as it moves toward fullness. In the same way, your efforts will begin to appear, little by little, as you work toward your goals.

It's important to remember that, just like the moon, your progress might not be obvious from one day to the next. If you look for change each night, you might not see much. But compare the razor-thin crescent at the start of the week to the quarter-moon a few days later, and the difference is clear. Growth happens gradually, then all at once.

In your journey, you'll also see a similar progression. From day to day, you may not be able to notice a significant difference in your level of progress; however, over time, you will see drastic changes have occurred as you keep working towards your goals.

The first steps are always the toughest. Old habits pull you back, comfort tries to keep you where you are, and starting something new feels awkward. This is where most big plans and New Year's resolutions go to die: people count on that first high-octane burst of motivation, but it never lasts over the long run. Motivation is quick to disappear, and it can't carry you all the way.

To navigate the Waxing Phases successfully, you need a more reliable source of energy than motivation. What will actually keep you moving forward are three core principles that govern all great achievement: **Consistency**, **Discipline**, and **Discretion**. These are the steady fuels that last long after the initial excitement wears off. In this chapter, we'll look at how to build these pillars into your daily life so you can keep moving toward your goals.

Consistency: The Engine of Greatness

The first pillar is **Consistency**. No one writes a bestselling novel in a weekend, and no skyscraper goes up overnight. Real success is built from steady, repeated effort, often in small, unglamorous steps. It's not a single event, but a process that unfolds over time. The truth is, most achievements are the result of showing up and doing the work, even when it feels boring or slow.

Our culture hates this idea. We are obsessed with the myth of the overnight success, the "get rich quick" schemes, and the quantum leaps that transform lives in an instant. We devour stories of entrepreneurs who "made it" seemingly out of nowhere, actors who were "discovered" at a coffee shop, or artists whose work "suddenly" went viral.

Unfortunately, this narrative is a fantasy 99.9% of the time. Many people play the lottery, but only a fraction of a percent of players will ever win a jackpot prize. Those who do win jackpot prizes are then highly unlikely to maintain their wealth, as they haven't built the skills necessary to manage it. With this being said, your chances of success are far greater in chasing a dream that you were meant to pursue than by playing games with impossible odds or waiting for lightning to strike.

But the truth is, what looks like sudden success is almost always built on countless small decisions and quiet effort behind the scenes. We see the highlight moments like the launch, the bestseller, or the championship, but we forget about the years of work and dedication that made them possible. It's like admiring the top of a mountain and forgetting about the massive foundation beneath it, built up layer by layer over time.

Consistency is the engine of compounding effort. It is the least sexy but most powerful force in the universe. Think of a stonecutter hammering away at a rock, perhaps a hundred times, without so much as a crack showing in it. Yet at the 101st blow, it splits in two. The stonecutter didn't hit it any harder the 101st time than the first 100 times; it was the cumulative pressure of the 100 previous strikes that caused the boulder to break.

People only notice the breakthrough moment when everything changes. But it's the many quiet, persistent efforts before that moment that really matter. Every small action is a step forward, even if it doesn't seem to make a difference right away. Your journey will feel the same way.

That's what consistency really looks like. It's not about big, dramatic moments. It's about showing up, even when you don't feel like it. It's writing a few hundred words when you'd rather do anything else, or making another call after a tough day. It's doing the basic work of practicing, learning, and repeating when no one is watching, and it doesn't feel exciting.

Jerry Seinfeld famously advised an aspiring comedian named Brad Isaac to build consistency in joke writing by ensuring that they wrote at least one joke every day.[22] To ensure that he wrote jokes daily, Seinfeld suggested that Isaac buy a wall calendar and a red marker. For each day Isaac completed his writing task, Seinfeld told them to write a big red X over that day. Eventually, this creates a "chain" of red X's on the calendar, which serves as a motivational tool to keep the streak going. As Seinfeld told Isaac, "Your only job is to not break the chain."
[22]

The genius of this method is that it isn't focused on writing a perfect joke; it's about establishing the consistent practice of writing daily. This level of consistency allows you to grow on a daily basis, and throughout just one Lunar Cycle, your level of growth will be exponential from start to finish.

When people think of Jerry Seinfeld, they see his success: the hit show, the fame, the fortune. What they don't see are the years of steady effort that made it all possible. Luck might open a door, but it's consistent effort that prepares you to walk through it when the time comes.

Systems for Achieving Consistency

The brilliance of Seinfeld's strategy is that it is not just a goal, but a system that helps you achieve it. As business consultant and author James Clear explains in his transformative book *Atomic Habits*, "You do not rise to the level of your goals. You fall to the level of your systems."[23] This is why you need to establish systems that help you maintain consistent progress towards your goals.

As we've discussed, a goal is nothing more than a desired outcome; it's the destination you want to reach. "I want to write a book" is a goal. "I want to lose 30 pounds" is a goal. "I want to start a successful business" is a goal. But relying on your goal for daily motivation is a losing strategy; hence the paradox of the New Year's Resolution.

A system, however, is entirely different. A system is the collection of daily habits and routines that will get you to that outcome. "I write 500 words every morning before breakfast" is a system. "I go to the gym every Monday, Wednesday, and Friday at 6 AM" is a system. "I make 10 sales calls every afternoon between 2-4 PM" is a system.

When you focus on your system, you get a win every time you stick to your routine. You don't have to wait for the big goal to feel successful. You're succeeding each day, just by showing up and doing the work.

The best way to stay consistent is to make it as easy as possible to show up. Here are a few simple strategies that can help:

Habit Stacking: This is the practice of linking a new habit to an existing one.[24] Your brain already has established neural pathways for your existing habits, so you can piggyback on that existing infrastructure. For example: "After I pour my morning coffee (existing habit), I will sit down and write for 30 minutes (new habit)." Or "After I brush my teeth at night (existing habit), I will do 10 push-ups (new habit)." The existing habit becomes the trigger for the new behavior, making it much more likely to stick.

Time Blocking: This means scheduling non-negotiable appointments with yourself for your most important work.[25] If your goal is to write, you block out 6:00-7:30 AM every Monday, Wednesday, and Friday on your calendar, and you treat that time as sacred. It should be as non-negotiable as a doctor's appointment or a meeting with your boss. You don't wait for motivation or "free time" to magically appear. You create the structure, and then you show up to fill it.

Environment Design: This is the principle of making good habits easy and bad habits hard, which is a foundational concept in James Clear's work in *Atomic Habits*.[26] If you want to work out in the morning, lay out your workout clothes the night before so they're the first thing you see when you wake up. If you want to eat healthier, don't keep junk food in your house, make the bad choice require extra effort (such as driving to the store). Meanwhile, if you keep healthy food available in your house, the good choice is effortless, as the fruit is sitting on the counter. Your environment should be designed to make your desired behavior the path of least resistance.

Real consistency, however, is about more than just habits; it's about who you become. Every time you take action, you're casting a vote for the kind of person you want to be. One day of writing makes you a writer for that day. Do it again tomorrow, and the day after, and soon you'll see yourself differently. Over time, your actions shape your identity.

This is the profound psychological shift that makes habits stick. When your actions match the person you want to be, it stops feeling like a struggle. Instead of thinking, "I should work on my project," you start to think, "This is just what I do." That's the real goal of the Waxing Phases: turning your ambition into part of who you are.

You can also keep track of your consistency through a systematic approach to keep yourself accountable. Below, I've included a simple method for tracking your consistency and momentum.

The Momentum Tracker

First, create a simple spreadsheet or journal with 3 daily entries:

1. Did I execute my systems today? (yes/no and a brief note)
2. What is my energy level? (scale of 1-10, 10 being fully-energized, 1 being fully-depleted)
3. What did I learn today? (brief note about what you learned)

Then on a weekly basis, evaluate your journal entries for the week and ask yourself:

- How many days did I execute my systems?
- What pattern do I see in my energy levels?
- What is working better than expected?
- Does anything require adjustment?

Making a journal entry daily with this information should take no more than 5 minutes, but it will provide you with invaluable data for your Waning Phase review later in the Lunar Cycle. It also keeps you on-track and enables you to catch any early warning signs that indicate one or more of your systems are not working effectively.

Staying Consistent Through the Middle Stint

Let's be honest: the excitement you felt at the start won't last forever. Sooner or later, the buzz fades, and the results you want still seem far away. This is the "Middle Stint:" the stretch between the first spark and the finish line. It's where most people give up, because motivation runs out, and only discipline keeps you going.

To understand what this feels like, I want you to step into the cockpit of a Formula 1 car and imagine what it's like to race at the highest level of motorsport.

The five red lights go out, and your world explodes in a symphony of roaring engines and wheelspin. The start of the race is pure adrenaline: the chaos of the first corner, twenty cars fighting for position, the thrill of overtaking in close-quarters combat with your competition. You're on top of your game, and you feel the most alive that you have ever felt. Your heart is pounding and your senses are heightened. Every choice you make matters.

Now, fast forward. You're in the lead. The end of the race is a clear and glorious destination you can almost taste: the final laps, the checkered flag, the champagne on the podium. It's starting to get in your head that you could take your team to victory today. The finish line is in sight. The win is within reach.

But now, it's lap 35 of 70. You're only halfway through the race. There's a 10-second gap to second place behind you, and you must focus on keeping your lap times consistent, hitting your marks, and managing your tires and fuel. There's no one in front of you to chase or battle wheel-to-wheel. No one is directly behind you, pressuring you, forcing you to defend. There may even be a pit stop required between now and the checkered flag. You can taste victory, but you also can't see the end of the race. Welcome to the middle stint.

The initial adrenaline has passed, and you now only feel the low hum of intense focus. Your tires, once fresh and full of grip, are starting to degrade. The car slides a little more on the exit of each corner. Your neck aches from the relentless G-forces that have been pulling at it for the last hour. Your body is screaming at you. The world outside the cockpit has shrunk to a hypnotic, grueling rhythm: find your braking point, bleed off the speed, turn in, hit the apex, squeeze the throttle, exit. Repeat. 20 times a lap. For the next hour.

This is where the race is truly won or lost. It's a valley of intense mental fatigue where the temptation to ease off, to miss an apex by an inch, or to brake a meter too early is a constant whisper in your ear. A few mistakes here and the outcome of your race could look dramatically different.

The key here is to expect this middle stretch and prepare for it. Hitting a plateau doesn't mean you're failing; it's just part of the process. The key isn't to push harder or hope for a burst of motivation. It's about changing how you approach the work and moving forward, one step at a time.

So, how do you do it? First, stop asking your race engineer for the gap to the car behind and refocus on what you can control inside the cockpit. You can't control what the other cars are doing, but you can control hitting the perfect apex on the very next corner. You can control your braking point at Turn 12. You can control managing your tire degradation by being smooth on the throttle. These micro-actions, these tiny optimizations, are entirely within your control, and they're the only things that matter right now.

Second, you must shift from focusing on the outcome to focusing on your process. You're not thinking about the podium right now. You're not even thinking about the end of this stint. You're thinking about this lap. This corner. This braking zone. You break the overwhelming task of "win the race" into the smallest possible unit: "execute this single action perfectly." And then you do it again, and again, and again.

Third, you fall in love with the process. You find beauty in the precision of hitting the same apex lap after lap. You find satisfaction in the consistency of your lap times. You find joy in the mastery of the small, repeatable acts of excellence that are entirely within your control. This is where champions are made: not in the dramatic overtakes or the thrilling starts, but in the quiet, relentless excellence of the middle stint.

Eventually, the checkered flag will wave, and you'll get to stand on the podium if you play your cards right. You just have to realize that a Grand Prix isn't won in a single lap. It's won over dozens of laps where consistency and world-class execution are crucial for a winning effort. Mastering consistency in the middle stint is what makes the difference between the greatest drivers in the world, such as Vettel, Schumacher, and Verstappen, and those who never contend for a Grand Prix win.

Your own journey is no different. Your championship is your *Orbiting Ambition*. Your Grand Prix is your Lunar Cycle, and a middle stint will appear in every single Lunar Cycle you undertake. Your success will not be born in a single moment. It will be forged in the quiet consistency of the middle stint: the thousand unglamorous choices you make to hit your apex, perfectly, every single day.

The middle stint is where you'll face your biggest tests. If you continue to follow your plan and adhere to your systems, you'll keep moving forward, and eventually, you'll see the results. But if you give in to doubt, you'll never know what you could have achieved.

Discipline: The Principle That Keeps You On-Course

If consistency keeps you moving, discipline keeps you on-course. Discipline isn't about punishing yourself or forcing your way through. It's about making smart choices and focusing on what matters most. Sometimes, it means saying no to good things so you can say yes to what's truly important.

Many people believe discipline is solely about willpower, pushing through obstacles regardless of the circumstances, much like an inner drill sergeant. But that approach doesn't work for long. Willpower wears out, just like a muscle.

Research from the American Psychological Association has shown that willpower is a finite resource that depletes throughout the day.[27] If you rely on willpower alone, you will eventually burn out. Each time you are tested throughout the day, the impact on your mental health increases, and you become less and less likely to have the willpower to work on something that you aren't required to do.

This is why it is crucial to build systems and rely on them to stay on track. If solid systems are in place, you aren't using willpower to extend yourself, but instead using discipline to ensure that you are relying on your system every day to contribute to your goal. For example, if you have a system in place to ride your Peloton daily (as I do), you won't feel like it's an "extra" thing to work out for 20 minutes after you get home from work. It's just something you do. You don't need motivation or extra willpower to do it; you just need discipline to stick to the system.

Furthermore, sustainable discipline isn't about running on empty. You can't be disciplined if you're exhausted. It's about making sure you have the energy you need to keep going.

A Formula 1 car can be the most advanced machine on the planet, engineered to perfection, but without fuel, fresh tires, and a well-rested driver to race it, the car is nothing more than an expensive piece of metal sitting in the garage. Your energy is your fuel, and your rest is your pit stop.

Before you can do the hard work of chasing your goals, you need to take care of your energy. That means focusing on the basics: getting enough sleep, eating well, and moving your body. These simple things make a big difference. I'm not here to lecture you about getting enough sleep or eating your vegetables; you already know what you need to do. But if you're trying to build something important while running on little sleep and junk food, you're making things much harder for yourself.

If your discipline slips, it's not because you're weak; it's because you're running on empty. The first step is to take care of your basic needs. Taking care of yourself is not a luxury, it's a necessity if you want to do your best work.

In my consulting career, I've had many projects that demanded extremely high levels of work, often tempting me to skip meals, forget to take my medications, and neglect to make time for exercise or rest. Every single time that I did this, however, I always ended up feeling ill, tired, and ready to lash out at the next person who asked me a question. While periods of intensity will occur, my point is that you must maintain your basic needs to do your best work. Nobody is going to admire a half-assed project; you need to bring your best self to work if you really want to achieve your goals.

Another key to discipline is to stop thinking you need to work for hours on end. No one can focus deeply for 8 or 12 hours straight. The best performers in every field, from athletes to programmers, have learned that our brains work best in cycles.

The most effective and creative people work in intense, focused bursts of around 90 minutes, followed by a genuine break.[28] Not a "check your email and social media" break, but a real one: a short walk, some stretching, a few minutes of quiet, maybe a brief conversation with a colleague about anything other than work.

Working in focused bursts, then taking genuine breaks, is the key to sustained performance. It's not about being busy all the time, but rather about being fully engaged when you work, and truly resting when you aren't actively working. That's what separates top performers from those who just slog through the day. When you take care of your energy, discipline becomes easier. The goal is to make good choices the easy ones, especially during those times when your willpower is low.

Think about that familiar 3 PM slump, when your energy dips and the craving for a quick sugar hit from the vending machine or a can of soda feels overwhelming. In that moment, your willpower is at its lowest. Your brain is tired from a morning of focused work. Your blood sugar might be dropping. Your stress levels are elevated. Relying on sheer grit to resist the temptation is a battle you will eventually lose. The smarter, more compassionate strategy is to have prepared for that moment in advance.

This is about being an architect of your environment. You use your well-rested, high-willpower brain in the morning to make a good decision for your tired, low-willpower brain in the afternoon. Instead of leaving it to chance, you pack healthy snacks like apples, almonds, and protein bars and put them on your desk in the morning. This makes them easier to reach than the candy down the hall.

You fill up a large water bottle or make a cup of green tea in anticipation of that afternoon's thirst, so you aren't as tempted by the soda machine. You schedule your most demanding creative work for the morning when your energy is highest, and you save the routine administrative tasks for the afternoon when your capacity is lower.

By planning ahead, you've set up guardrails for your future self. This isn't about being strict; it's about being smart. When you prepare for the tough moments in advance, you save your willpower for the challenges that really matter. Instead of fighting yourself, you've created an environment that helps you succeed.

Discretion: The Art of Strategic Silence

The third and final pillar of the Waxing Phases is the most subtle, but in many ways, the most important. It is the art of **Discretion**. It is the wisdom of knowing what to share, with whom, and when.

In our culture of oversharing, where social media has trained us to broadcast every thought, every meal, and every milestone to the world, the default behavior is to announce our grand plans to anyone who will listen. However, this is a strategic blunder that can derail your mission before it even takes off.

Studies have shown that when you announce a goal and receive social praise for it, your brain gets a small hit of dopamine that is similar to the dopamine you'd get from actually achieving the goal.[29]

This phenomenon reveals a troubling truth: discussing your goals can trick your brain into feeling a premature sense of accomplishment. You get the social validation and positive responses from friends and family, and your brain interprets this as progress. The result? Your motivation to do the actual hard work subtly decreases. You've already gotten the reward of social recognition without putting in the effort.

The danger of premature disclosure, however, goes far beyond this neurological quirk. Announcing your plans prematurely opens yourself up to a flood of unsolicited opinions, well-meaning but often misguided advice, and the projections of other people's fears onto your vision. This creates the potential for you to change your plans based on the opinions of those who don't understand your *Orbiting Ambition*.

Let's talk about several archetypes of dream killers you may encounter along your journey:

The Pessimist, who has never taken a big risk themselves and will tell you all the reasons why your idea can't work, projecting their own fear of failure onto your mission. "That's been tried before and it failed." "The market is too saturated." "You don't have the right background for that."

The Worrier, usually a parent or close friend who loves you and doesn't want to see you get hurt, so they counsel you toward the safe, conventional path. "Why would you leave your stable job for that?" "Wouldn't it be smarter to wait a few more years?" "I just don't want you to be disappointed."

The Uninformed Expert, who has just enough knowledge to be dangerous but not enough to be helpful, and will confidently give you a map to a completely different territory than the one you're trying to navigate. They'll tell you what worked for them or for someone they heard about, without understanding that your mission, your context, and your capabilities are unique.

The Silent Destroyer, who is secretly intimidated by your ambition because it makes them uncomfortable about their own lack of progress, and will plant subtle seeds of doubt disguised as concern. "Are you sure you're ready for that?" "I'd hate to see you burn out." "You seem really stressed, maybe you should take a break."

Even people who care about you can add doubt and confusion. They might make you question your decisions or push you to compromise your vision. In the early stages, when your idea is still taking shape, outside doubts can be especially damaging.

This principle of strategic silence is a proven strategy of the highest performers across every domain. Look at Apple under Steve Jobs. Their culture of secrecy was legendary, and it wasn't just to prevent competitors from stealing their ideas; it was also to protect their own innovations. It was to protect the fragile creative process from the crushing pressure of public expectation and uninformed criticism. They could iterate, they could fail privately, they could change direction without having to explain themselves to the world. The product only went public when it was ready, when it had been refined, and when it could stand on its own and speak for itself.[30]

Being discreet doesn't mean keeping everything to yourself. It's about being thoughtful about who you share your ideas with, and when. The key is to choose your inner circle wisely and share your progress at the right time.

Curating Your Inner Circle

First, you must become the ruthless curator of your inner circle. Think about the people you are closest to, the ones you naturally turn to when you want to share news or seek advice. When you share a fragile, new idea with them, what happens?

Do they offer thoughtful questions that help you stress-test and strengthen your thinking? Do they challenge you in ways that make you sharper and more prepared? Or do they immediately poke holes in it, listing all the reasons why it won't work? Do they deflate your energy with their skepticism or their worry?

There is a profound difference between a supporter who stress-tests your plans because they want you to succeed and they want your plan to be as strong as possible, and a doubter who sows seeds of negativity, whether through well-meaning "advice" or intentional sabotage. You need to be able to distinguish between these two types of feedback.

A true supporter might say: "I love this idea. Have you thought about how you'll handle X challenge? What's your plan if Y happens?" They're not trying to discourage you; they're trying to prepare you. They believe in you and your mission, but they're also realistic about the obstacles you'll face. This is the kind of feedback that makes your plan stronger.

A doubter, on the other hand, might say: "I don't know, that sounds really risky. Are you sure you know what you're doing? What if it doesn't work out? You have so much to lose." They're not offering solutions or helping you prepare; they're amplifying your fears and making you question whether you should even try.

You don't need people who just agree with everything you say. What you need are supporters who believe in you, challenge you to grow, and genuinely want to see you succeed.

A simple rule of thumb is to surround yourself with people who are playing a bigger game than you are. Someone who has already achieved the level of success you're striving for is far less likely to tear you down out of their own insecurity. They've been where you are. They know the journey. They can offer wisdom without judgment.

If the people closest to you put down your dreams or make you feel small, it's time to rethink who you share your ideas with. You don't have to cut anyone out, but you can stop looking for their approval. Instead, find mentors and supporters who understand your journey and want to help you grow.

This is about protecting yourself and your goals. Your inner circle should be your advisors, not your doubters. When you trust the people around you, you can share your progress with confidence.

"Walk the Walk" before "Talking the Talk"

Once you have the right people in your orbit, the next layer of discretion is about timing. For this, I want you to adopt a simple but powerful guiding principle: **talk about what you have done, not what you are going to do**. Or, as it is often said, "Walk the walk before you talk the talk."

As we previously discussed, there is a subtle psychological trap in announcing your grand plans before you've taken any action. Sharing your intention to write a book, start a company, or launch a product can give you a small, satisfying hit of social validation; a little dopamine reward that feels a lot like actual accomplishment.

People say "Wow, that's amazing!" or "I can't wait to see that!" and your brain interprets this as progress. This prematurely releases the tension that is meant to fuel your work, making you less likely to actually do the hard work of execution.

But if you keep your plans to yourself and focus on the work, you'll only get recognition when you've actually made progress. This keeps your motivation strong and your focus where it belongs.

This doesn't mean you can't talk to anyone about your ideas. It just means it's better to take the first step before you announce your plans. Let your actions speak first.

Then, when you do share, talk about what you've accomplished. Tell your inner circle about the chapter you finished, the client you landed, or the streak you've built. Share your progress, not just your intentions.

This does two things: it gives you recognition and accountability after you've earned it, and it builds trust with the people you share it with. When you follow through on your promises, people notice. They see you as someone who takes action, not just someone who talks. If you show progress before you share, you become a doer, not just a dreamer.

Once you have something real to show (your Full Moon moment), you can share your story more widely and invite others in. But in the early stages, protect your mission by keeping it close until it's ready.

To understand why this principle of earned disclosure is so critical, let me share a parable that illustrates the danger of projecting an image of success you haven't actually earned.

As an avid watch enthusiast, I have always wanted to purchase a Rolex. These watches are iconic symbols of success and craftsmanship. It would be very tempting to go out and buy a "knock-off" that looks like a real one at a fraction of the cost. It would fool most people and give me the illusion of the social status that comes with that iconic Rolex Crown logo. But here's the problem: I would know it's a fake. The people who really know watches, the true enthusiasts and collectors, would spot it instantly. I would be promoting an image of success I hadn't actually earned yet, and anyone who had achieved that level of success would instantly spot me as an imposter.

Beyond the risk of being exposed as an imposter, there is a danger that is likely even greater: if the day finally came that I could afford a genuine Rolex, the moment would be cheapened by the premature dopamine hit that I stole by wearing the fake. The people I tried to fool wouldn't be impressed when I got the real one, because they thought I already had one. Or even worse, I might become so satisfied with the unearned social status that I'd lose the motivation to chase the real goal. The fake would have robbed me of the drive to earn the real thing.

You are far better off wearing a genuine $30 Casio than a fake Rolex. With the Casio, you are being authentic. You are exactly who you claim to be. You're wearing a watch that matches your current station in life, and there's no shame in that. You're not pretending to be something you're not. With the fake Rolex, you're an imposter who likely isn't fooling anyone that you'd like to impress.

To be clear, this idea isn't about watches, money, or material possessions. It's about the fundamental principle of earned authenticity. It's a fantastic goal to aspire to owning a Rolex, a Corvette, or a mansion. It's also a fantastic goal to want to write a book, start a company, or earn an advanced degree. But projecting that the goal is finished before you've actually started is like wearing a fake watch; it steals the joy from the real achievement. It gives you unearned status. It robs you of the motivation to do the actual work.

If you want real success, make discretion part of your approach. Choose carefully who you share your ideas with, and wait until you've made real progress. Do the work quietly, and celebrate publicly when you have something genuine to show. Let the world see the real result, not just the dream.

The Three Pillars Working in Concert: The Dyson Story

These three pillars — Consistency, Discipline, and Discretion — are the bedrock of the Waxing Phases. However, to see how they come together to create something truly monumental, it is instructive to examine one of the greatest stories of "the grind" in modern history: the invention of the Dyson vacuum cleaner. This is an incredible story that was featured on one of my favorite podcasts, *How I Built This*, and I highly recommend listening to this episode.[31]

Today, James Dyson is a billionaire and a universal symbol of British innovation and engineering excellence. His company revolutionized an entire industry, and his products are in millions of homes around the world, including my own. But his success was not born from a single flash of genius, and it certainly wasn't an overnight success story. It was forged in a brutal, relentless, and lonely set of Waxing Phases that lasted for five full years: a masterclass in consistency, discipline, and discretion.

The story began with a moment of righteous anger, which we discussed back in Chapter 1. Dyson was frustrated with his expensive, top-of-the-line Hoover vacuum, which constantly clogged and lost suction. This was a problem everyone else accepted as a normal, inevitable flaw in the design of vacuum cleaners.

For Dyson, however, it was an infuriating design flaw that shouldn't exist. His *Orbiting Ambition* was born in that moment of frustration: to create a radically better vacuum cleaner that would never lose suction, solve his problem, and revolutionize the vacuum cleaner industry.

His New Moon phase was a period of intense research and learning. He became obsessed with industrial cyclonic separators used in sawmills to remove dust from the air. These massive machines used centrifugal force to separate particles without the need for filters that could clog. He formed a hypothesis: could a miniature version of this technology be adapted for use in a domestic vacuum cleaner? With his blueprint in hand, informed by physics and engineering principles, he entered his Waxing Phases.

He began building prototypes in a small shed behind his house. His first prototype was a crude contraption made of cardboard and tape, but it proved the basic concept could work. The cyclone could generate enough suction to pick up dust, and it didn't lose power as a bag would. This was his first small win, which served as the initial spark that fueled the long journey ahead.

What followed was a masterclass in **consistency**. He spent the next five years of his life in that shed, methodically building one prototype after another, testing and refining in an endless cycle of experimentation. His process was the very definition of the aggregation of marginal gains.

Each new prototype would test one small variable: the angle of the cyclone, the diameter of the opening, the material used for construction, and the placement of the motor. Most of the experiments failed. The cyclone wouldn't generate enough suction. Or it would work, but it was too loud. Or it was the right volume, but it cost too much to manufacture. But each failure provided a new piece of data, a small lesson that informed the next iteration.

His wife, a teacher, supported their family with her modest salary while he pursued this dream. He sank deeper and deeper into personal debt, borrowing against his house, maxing out credit cards, doing whatever it took to fund the next prototype. This was his middle stint, a period that lasted not for weeks or months, but for years. The initial excitement had long since faded. The support from friends and family had turned to concern and even criticism. He had no investors, no team, no public validation of his vision.

He took his concept to all the major vacuum manufacturers and pitched his revolutionary design to them. They all rejected him. They told him his idea was too expensive, too complex, and that there was no market for a premium vacuum cleaner. Some of them even laughed him out of the room. These were the dream killers we discussed earlier, and they could have easily discouraged James Dyson and prevented one of the greatest success stories in business from being possible.

What kept him going? It was a system built on the three pillars:

His **consistency** was legendary: he showed up to the shed every single day, even when he had no idea if he was getting closer to a solution, even when he wanted to quit, even when the people he loved were begging him to stop and get a "real job."

His **discipline** was absolute: he said "no" to quitting, "no" to the chorus of rejection, and "no" to taking an easier path or compromising his vision, even when his financial situation was dire and his family's future was on the line.

His **discretion** was total: he worked in relative obscurity, perfecting his invention without the pressure of public announcements, investor expectations, or the need to prove himself to critics. He didn't announce his plans to the world. He didn't seek validation. He just worked.

After five years and an astonishing 5,127 prototypes, he finally had it: the world's first bagless vacuum cleaner that didn't lose suction. Prototype 5,127 worked. It worked beautifully. This was his Full Moon. He had created a product so demonstrably superior to every competitor on the market that it would go on to disrupt an entire industry, making him one of the wealthiest people in Britain and establishing his company as a global brand synonymous with innovation and quality.

But that spectacular success, that brilliant Full Moon that the world now sees, was only possible because of the five years of dark, lonely, relentless work in "the grind." His story is the ultimate testament to the power of the Waxing Phases. It is a reminder that the greatest breakthroughs are not the result of a single moment of inspiration, but the product of thousands of moments of unwavering consistency, ironclad discipline, and strategic discretion. It's proof that if you can master these three pillars, there is no limit to what you can build.

By now, it's clear that the Waxing Phases are not glamorous. No one will write headlines about your early mornings or late nights, or the quiet work you do when no one is watching. This isn't the part that makes you famous.

But this is where you shape your future. In the Waxing Phases, you prove to yourself what you can do. You're not just building a project; you're building your character, your identity, and your belief in your own ability to finish what you start.

⑦

Managing Tidal Forces
and Lunar Eclipses

As we discussed, the Waxing Phases aren't exactly full of glamour and fame; in fact, you'll usually experience a lot of unglamourous decisions that you'll be forced to make alone. With that being said, the *Lunar Phase Framework* isn't a guarantee that everything will go according to plan, and sometimes, you'll have to make difficult decisions to engage with the reality of life as it unfolds.

It's tempting to imagine that you can chart your progress like a perfect lunar calendar; setting New Moon intentions, building Waxing momentum, celebrating at the Full Moon, and reflecting during the Waning Phases, all right on schedule. But life doesn't operate on a fixed timetable, and the tides don't wait for your permission to rise or fall. The world keeps moving, no matter what you're working toward. Reality, with all its unpredictability, is always just around the corner.

Reality is the unpredictable element in your Lunar Cycle. Sometimes, all it takes is a single phone call, an unexpected storm, or a crisis that appears overnight to send your plans spinning. Other times, it's a gradual process, a slow but steady leak of energy that you barely notice until it's gone. Then, there are the eclipses, when everything seems to go dark and you're left in a space of uncertainty, unsure of what comes next.

We call these disruptions Tidal Forces and Lunar Eclipses, because they are as much a part of our cycles as the moon's own shadow. The real question isn't whether they'll show up, but how you'll respond when they do.

In this chapter, we'll explore how to navigate both the slow-building pressures and the sudden storms that can throw you off-course. You'll learn how to tell the difference between challenges you can manage with small adjustments and those that call for a complete change of direction.

The aim isn't just to get through tough times, but to understand what kind of challenge you're facing and respond in a way that protects your long-term goals and your well-being. Sometimes that means pushing forward; other times, it means pausing, regrouping, and finding your footing again after life has knocked you sideways. Regardless of the disruption you face, the most important piece is that you don't let it stop you from achieving your *Orbiting Ambition*.

Two Disruptors: Tidal Forces and Lunar Eclipses

Not all disruptions are the same. Some are frustrating and exhausting, but you can work through them using the systems you already have in place. Others are much bigger and represent events that can change your path entirely. Knowing the difference matters because each one calls for a different kind of response.

Tidal Forces are the constant, predictable stresses that pull at your momentum. They're the everyday pressures that accumulate gradually: an overwhelming workload, interpersonal conflicts, financial strain, health issues that simmer rather than explode. These forces don't arrive suddenly; they build over time, exerting a steady gravitational pull that can slowly drag you off-course if you're not paying attention.

Think about ocean tides. They're powerful, relentless, and entirely predictable if you understand the how they work. You can plan around them based on the time of day, and at times, you can use them to your advantage. But if you ignore them, you'll find yourself fighting against a force you can't overcome through sheer effort alone. You'll get pulled into the ocean before you even realize what is happening.

The same is true of the Tidal Forces in your life. An unhealthy work environment doesn't usually destroy you in a single day; it erodes your energy and motivation over months. A strained relationship doesn't typically implode overnight; it deteriorates through the accumulation of unaddressed conflicts. Financial pressure doesn't bankrupt you instantly; it compounds through small decisions that seem manageable in isolation but become overwhelming when considered collectively.

The real risk with Tidal Forces is how easy they are to accept as normal. You adjust to the pressure bit-by-bit, until what would have seemed impossible six months ago now feels routine. It's easy to tell yourself you're managing, when in reality, you're just getting used to treading water.

Lunar Eclipses, on the other hand, are sudden, dramatic events that temporarily obscure everything. They're the crises that arrive without warning and demand immediate attention: a serious illness or injury, the sudden loss of a job, a relationship ending, a family emergency, a global pandemic, a natural disaster, a business failure, a profound personal loss.

These aren't gradual erosions, they're ruptures. They don't just challenge your current cycle; they call into question whether you can continue at all. During a Lunar Eclipse, your carefully planned New Moon becomes irrelevant, your Waxing Phase momentum stops dead, and your ability to even think about your *Orbiting Ambition* vanishes behind the immediate crisis demanding all your attention.

The key difference is that Tidal Forces require management and adjustment. Lunar Eclipses require survival and adaptation. Tidal Forces can be navigated using your existing framework with some modifications. Lunar Eclipses may force you to temporarily abandon the framework entirely while you deal with the crisis, then rebuild afterward.

Understanding what you're facing is the first step to responding effectively.

Navigating Tidal Forces: Strategic Adjustment

Let me tell you about a period when I experienced the compounding weight of Tidal Forces. Over the course of three months, I dealt with a severe respiratory illness that lasted weeks, a business trip through a hurricane that stranded me away from home, a week without power or running water, a broken water heater in winter, a mysterious foot injury that required medical attention, and ultimately, having to make the heartbreaking decision to put my childhood dog to sleep.

Each event by itself would have been manageable. Annoying, painful, and draining, but survivable. Combined, they created a compound effect that threatened to completely derail my momentum. I was still trying to maintain my work commitments, honor my personal goals, and run a political campaign while feeling like I was drowning in an endless series of setbacks.

This is what makes Tidal Forces so challenging. They rarely show up one at a time, neatly spaced out so you can handle each in turn. Instead, they pile up, overlap, and make everything feel heavier. And while you're dealing with them, the rest of life doesn't pause to give you a break. As the saying goes, "when it rains, it pours."

What I've learned is that trying to fight Tidal Forces head-on is exhausting and rarely works. The better approach is to notice them early, be honest about what's happening, and make thoughtful adjustments to your framework so you can keep moving forward, even when the pressure is high.

The Early Warning System

The first line of defense against Tidal Forces is noticing them before they overwhelm you. This requires building an early warning system to detect when the pressure is building to unsustainable levels. Here are three areas that indicate Tidal Forces are growing:

1. **Energy Deficit:** Am I consistently ending each day more exhausted than I started it? Am I relying increasingly on caffeine, willpower, or sheer grit to get through basic tasks? If yes, I'm likely experiencing Tidal Forces that are draining my reserves faster than I can replenish them.

2. **Emotional Volatility:** Am I more irritable, more anxious, more prone to frustration or tears? Am I losing my sense of humor about things that wouldn't normally bother me? Emotional volatility is often the first visible sign that underlying pressures are exceeding my capacity to manage them.

3. **System Degradation:** Are the habits and routines that normally sustain me starting to slip? Am I skipping workouts, eating poorly, sleeping irregularly, missing deadlines, or letting communication lag? When my systems start failing despite my best intentions, it's usually because the load on those systems has exceeded their design capacity.

Anytime you notice one of these indicators is increasing, you should pay attention. If you notice two, it's time to take action. If you notice all three, you're in the midst of significant Tidal Forces and need to make immediate adjustments to weather the storm.

The most important thing is to notice these signals early, before they turn into full-blown crises. Most of us don't realize we're in trouble until we're already underwater, and by then, the changes we need to make are much harder and more disruptive.

While the following sections will dive more deeply into how to navigate Tidal Forces and Lunar Eclipses, here is an easy tool you can use to decide if you are undergoing Tidal Forces, Lunar Eclipses, or just normal friction that you can push through. I call it the **Eclipse Navigation Matrix.**

Eclipse Navigation Matrix

Take out a piece of paper and draw a 4x4 matrix. In the top-left, label it "**Normal Friction.**" This quadrant will house all of the things you're going through that you can categorize as normal stressors that you can push through. In the bottom-left, you'll label the quadrant as "**Warning Sign.**" This will be where you'll write any of the warning signs that indicate Tidal Forces may be coming, which you will need to monitor closely.

On the top-right, you'll label this quadrant "**Tidal Force,**" and this is where you'll list any Tidal Forces that are already upon you. Here is where you'll need to adjust and adapt to the current situation. Finally, the bottom-right quadrant will be labeled "**Lunar Eclipse,**" and this is where you'll list any Lunar Eclipses that currently have you in survival mode.

Take a look at **Figure 4** on the next page for an illustration of how this should look. You'll also notice additional labeling of "Low/High Severity" and "Temporary/Persistent." This is because Normal Friction and Warning Signs are not severe in the sense of disrupting your Lunar Cycle, while Tidal Forces and Lunar Eclipses are extremely disruptive.

Additionally, Normal Friction and Tidal Forces are viewed as temporary, as they will end once they have run their course. Meanwhile, Warning Signs and Lunar Eclipses are more persistent. Warning Signs continuously tell you something is wrong, and Lunar Eclipses completely disrupt your Lunar Cycle. These will also run their course, but they may take longer to do so and require more action from you to resolve.

The Eclipse Navigation Matrix orbiting ambition

	Low Severity	High Severity
Temporary	*Normal Friction* (Push Through)	*Tidal Force* (Adjust & Adapt)
Persistent	*Warning Sign* (Monitor Closely)	*Lunar Eclipse* (Survival Mode)

Figure 4: The Eclipse Navigation Matrix

I highly recommend that you use this tool whenever you're facing potential Tidal Forces and Lunar Eclipses. The simple act of sorting out all of your stressors can help you significantly in identifying the true impact of what you are encountering, and it gives you a clear outline of what you need to focus on resolving first to get back to working towards your Orbiting Ambition.

The Pressure Valve Principle

Once you've identified that you're experiencing significant Tidal Forces, you need to release pressure before it ruptures your entire system. This means deliberately choosing what to let go of temporarily.

This is counterintuitive for ambitious people. We're trained to believe that success comes from persevering through difficulty, from refusing to quit, from maintaining all commitments no matter what. But there's a crucial difference between perseverance and stubbornness: perseverance means continuing to pursue your *Orbiting Ambition* even when it's difficult, while stubbornness means refusing to adjust your tactics even when they're clearly not working.

During that three-month period, I had to make difficult choices about what to maintain and what to release. I couldn't keep every commitment and meet every goal at the same level while simultaneously dealing with a constant stream of emergencies. Something had to give.

Here's a set of steps you can take to decide what you need to do to release your pressure valve:

1. **Protect the Foundation:** Identify the absolute minimum required to keep your life functional and your health intact. This typically includes: getting enough sleep to function, eating adequately (even if not optimally), maintaining your primary income source, and preserving your most critical relationships. These are non-negotiable. Everything else is on the table for adjustment.

2. **Pause the Side-Projects:** Identify which goals and projects can be temporarily suspended without permanent damage. This might mean putting a side business on hold, skipping a few gym sessions, postponing a creative project, or letting housework slide for a few weeks. The key piece of this phrase is **temporarily**. You're not quitting; you're pausing. You'll restart when conditions improve.

3. **Simplify the Systems:** Reduce your existing systems to their most essential elements. If your morning routine normally includes meditation, journaling, exercise, and reading, maybe you keep just the meditation and exercise. If your work system

119

includes multiple projects, maybe you try to focus on just the highest-impact one.

4. **Communicate the Constraints:** Be honest with the people who depend on you about what you're dealing with and what adjustments you're making. Most people are remarkably understanding when you explain you're going through a difficult period and need to temporarily reduce your availability or output. What damages relationships is disappearing without explanation or continuing to commit to things you can't deliver.

While undergoing the brunt of Tidal Forces, I applied this framework ruthlessly. I protected my sleep, my core work commitments, and my closest relationships. I paused several personal projects I'd been excited about. I communicated to friends and colleagues that I was in survival mode and asked for grace.

Did this feel like failure? Absolutely. Every part of me that wanted to keep pushing resisted making these changes. But what I discovered is that pulling back for a while isn't the same as giving up.

By intentionally letting go of some things, I avoided a total collapse. I kept moving forward, even if it was at a slower pace than I had hoped. And when things finally eased up, I could pick up where I left off, instead of having to start over from scratch.

The Recalibration Process

Once you've released immediate pressure, you need to recalibrate your expectations and timelines. Tidal Forces don't just slow you down, they change the terrain you're navigating. What seemed achievable under normal conditions may not be achievable under current constraints.

This is where many people make a critical mistake: they hold themselves to the same standards they set when conditions were favorable, then beat themselves up for not meeting them. This is the worst-case scenario because it adds psychological pressure to already overwhelming practical pressure.

Instead, you need to explicitly recalibrate. During your next New Moon planning session, ask yourself:

- **What is actually possible right now?** This isn't what you wish were possible, nor is it what should be possible if everything were normal. The answer to this should be the things that are genuinely achievable given current constraints. Be brutally honest. If you're dealing with significant personal stress, your capacity is reduced. Acknowledge it. Plan accordingly.

- **What is the minimum viable progress?** You can't maintain full speed, but you can maintain direction. What's the smallest amount of progress that keeps you pointed toward your *Orbiting Ambition* without exceeding your current capacity?

- **What support do I need?** Tidal Forces often require external assistance to navigate. Can you hire help? Delegate tasks? Ask friends or family for specific support? Seek professional help (therapy, coaching, medical care)? Many people try to handle everything alone because they don't want to be a burden on others; however, isolation under pressure often turns manageable situations into crises.

- **What can I learn from this?** Tidal Forces are miserable, but they're also revealing. They show you what's truly essential versus what's merely habitual. They expose weak points in your systems. They clarify what matters most when you're forced to choose. Pay attention to these lessons, as they'll make your framework stronger when conditions improve.

During that tough period, I had to be honest with myself: my usual productivity goals just weren't realistic for a while. So, I adjusted my expectations. Instead of criticizing myself for doing less, I focused on whether I was making the best progress I could, given the circumstances. Shifting from rigid standards to ones that fit my reality helped me stay motivated and kept me from falling into the trap of self-blame.

Surviving Lunar Eclipses: When Everything Goes Dark

Tidal Forces can be managed with the right adjustments and strategies. Lunar Eclipses are a different story. These aren't challenges you work through; they're storms you simply have to survive.

A Lunar Eclipse is when something so significant happens that your normal framework becomes temporarily irrelevant. You're not planning a New Moon; you're in crisis mode. You're not executing Lunar Cycles; you're just trying to get through the day. Your *Orbiting Ambition* doesn't disappear, but it recedes so far into the background that you can barely remember what it felt like to care about long-term goals.

I've experienced several Lunar Eclipses in my life. Serious illness. Loss of loved ones. Career setbacks. Relationship endings. Each time, the systems I had built so carefully seemed to dissolve at once. The discipline I'd cultivated felt useless. The clarity I'd achieved vanished behind a wall of pain, confusion, or fear.

What I've learned is that when you're in the middle of a Lunar Eclipse, you can't expect yourself to keep up with your usual routines. Instead, you need to switch to a different approach: one that's focused on getting through and finding stability, rather than pushing for growth.

The Eclipse Protocol

When a Lunar Eclipse hits, your only goals are:

- **Stay Alive.** This sounds dramatic, but it's literal. Some Lunar Eclipses, such as serious illness, profound grief, and acute mental health crises, genuinely threaten your basic functioning. Your first priority is physical and mental survival. Eat something, even if it's not optimal. Sleep, even if it means taking medication or breaking your normal routine. Seek medical or therapeutic help if needed. Stay connected to people who care about you, even when isolation feels easier.

- **Protect Your Core Relationships.** Lunar Eclipses strain relationships because you're not yourself, you can't show up the way you normally would, and you need more support than you can reciprocate. Be honest with the people who matter

122

about what you're dealing with and what you need. Let them help if they offer. Forgive yourself for not being able to give as much as you normally would. The people who truly care about you will understand.

- **Do the Absolute Minimum Professionally.** Figure out what you *must* do to maintain your income and core professional obligations, then do only that. Everything else waits. Don't try to keep up appearances. Don't try to maintain your normal output. Don't judge yourself for being less productive. You're in survival mode; productivity is not the priority.

- **Let Everything Else Go.** All your ambitious goals, impressive projects, and carefully designed systems go on hold. Not forever, just until the Lunar Eclipse passes. You're not abandoning them; you're acknowledging that, right now, you don't have the capacity to care for them. And that's okay.

Following this protocol isn't a sign of weakness; it's a sign of wisdom. Sometimes, the best thing you can do is pull back for a while, so you don't break under the strain. Choosing to simplify for now is what keeps you from falling apart completely.

The Recovery Period

The hardest part of an eclipse isn't the initial impact; it's the recovery. The impact of Lunar Eclipses typically isn't resolved quickly. Recovery has its own timeline, and that timeline often exceeds your patience for it.

You can't rush grief. You can't force recovery from illness. You can't accelerate the rebuilding process after a major setback. You can only endure and trust that, like every Lunar Eclipse in history, this one will eventually pass.

During this period, it's easy to want to jump back into your old routines too soon. You might have a good day and think you're in the clear, only to find yourself struggling again the next. It's normal to feel frustrated about how long recovery takes or to compare yourself to others who seem to recover faster. You might even question your own strength, given that you're still having a hard time.

Try to let go of those worries. Healing takes its own time, and you can't rush it without making things harder in the long run. Your job right now isn't to speed things up, but to let the process unfold and take care of yourself as best you can.

What helps during this phase:

Lowered Expectations. Accept that you're in a different mode of operation and stop judging yourself by normal standards. You're not failing; you're healing. Those are different processes.

Small Victories. Celebrate getting through the day. Celebrate moments of normalcy. Celebrate any evidence that you're slowly improving. Progress during an eclipse is measured in inches, not miles.

Connection. Stay in contact with people who care about you, even when you don't feel like it. Isolation intensifies Lunar Eclipses. Connection, even an uncomfortable connection, provides the counterweight that keeps you tethered.

Perspective. Remember that every Lunar Eclipse in your life eventually comes to an end, and this one will too. You don't have to believe it right now, but somewhere in the back of your mind, hold space for the possibility that you will feel normal again, that the sun will return, and that this is temporary (even though it doesn't feel that way).

The Re-emergence Process

Eventually, the Lunar Eclipse lifts. Not suddenly, but gradually. You'll have more good days than bad. You'll notice you can think about the future again without it feeling overwhelming. You'll realize you've gone hours or even days without the crisis dominating your thoughts. You'll feel, tentatively, like maybe you're going to be okay.

This is a sensitive time. You're starting to recover, but you're not all the way back yet. If you try to jump straight into your old pace, you might find yourself overwhelmed again. Coming back requires its own careful, intentional process.

Take this time to review your *Orbiting Ambition* and revisit your Waning Phases. Acknowledge the impact of the Lunar Eclipse and decide what you truly want to work towards once you return to normal. Then, start small by re-establishing some of your productive habits, such as your workout routine. Begin to rebuild trust in yourself by making commitments slowly, and get yourself ready to execute your next Lunar Cycle.

Each restart should be intentional and paced, allowing you to rebuild momentum without overwhelming your still-recovering system. If you start with intention and grace, you'll be back to your normal self more quickly than if you attempt to dive in all at once. Even if your goals change, that is completely fine; when your reality changes, your plan needs to adapt. That's why The *Lunar Phase Framework* is designed to be agile.

The Physics of Recovery

It's important to remember that recovery from Tidal Forces and Lunar Eclipses doesn't happen in a straight line. You won't always feel a little better every single day. There will be setbacks that feel like you're moving backward, and good days that make you think you're done, only to be followed by tougher days.

This is completely normal. It doesn't mean you're doing anything wrong or that you won't recover. Healing just has its own rhythm, and it's often messier than the steady progress of growth.

Think of it like this: when you're building something new during normal conditions, you're working in one direction with momentum behind you. When you're recovering from disruption, you're working against multiple forces simultaneously: you're healing the damage, relearning lost skills, rebuilding confidence, and restoring systems. It takes longer and feels harder because it is harder.

But it's also possible. Every setback you've survived in the past is proof that you can survive this one. Every Lunar Eclipse that felt permanent eventually passed. Every Tidal Force that seemed overwhelming eventually subsided.

Your goal isn't to be immune to these forces. Instead, it's to build a framework that can bend without breaking, and that's strong enough to help you rebuild if things do fall apart. The *Lunar Phase Framework* offers that kind of structure not by keeping disruption away, but by giving you a way to move through it and come out of the other side with your ambitions still in orbit.

There will be times when everything feels uncertain or progress stalls completely. That's a natural part of any journey, not a sign that you've failed. When things are difficult, focus on taking care of yourself and holding steady. Trust that clarity and momentum will return, even if you can't see how yet. When they do, you'll be able to move forward with new insight and resilience, and you will be stronger because of what you've made it through.

⑧

The Full Moon

The hard, sometimes exhausting work of the Waxing Phases has finally brought you to this point. After moving through darkness and watching the light slowly grow, you've reached the Full Moon. This is the moment when the moon stands out in the night sky, fully visible and impossible to ignore. It's the point where all your planning, consistency, and discipline come together. You've "found your moon," and the goals you set back in the quiet of the New Moon phase are now real. Maybe your project is live, your book is in your hands, your business has its first real customers, or you've crossed the finish line. The work you did when no one was watching is now out in the open, shining for everyone to see.

Picture the feeling. For an entrepreneur, it's that first real order from someone you've never met. For a writer, it's holding your book for the first time, the weight of it proof of all those hours spent alone at your desk. For an athlete, it's the moment you cross the finish line, lungs burning, crowd cheering, and you realize you've arrived. It's a rush of relief, pride, excitement, and sometimes, a little fear. You've made it. So, what comes next?

Arriving at the Full Moon isn't the finish line; it's the beginning of a new phase. This stage brings its own challenges and fresh opportunities. The grit and drive that got you here won't be enough by themselves anymore. Before, your job was to build. Now, it's about managing, improving, and caring for what you've created. In this chapter, we'll look at how to make the most of this bright, sometimes complicated, part of your journey.

The Neurochemistry of Victory: Celebration Science

The first thing to do in this new phase is simple: celebrate. When you reach your goal, pause and take a moment to truly appreciate it. Too often, we skip past our wins, already thinking about what's next. But if you don't take time to celebrate, you miss a crucial step. Recognizing your success isn't just a feel-good bonus; it's a vital part of building real motivation and setting yourself up for what comes next.

You don't see a winning race car driver in any series win a race without taking a moment to celebrate at the end. You don't see a football team win a game without a post-game celebration. While it's essential to stay focused throughout a full season, without celebrating individual wins, it is impossible to maintain a high enough morale for the team to continue succeeding. Similarly, you must take the time to celebrate your win and allow yourself to reap the reward for all of your hard work.

To understand why, you need to understand what's happening in your brain. The entire journey through the Waxing Phases has been a process of delayed gratification. You put in the hard work, fueled by a belief that it would eventually lead to a worthwhile outcome. The moment of success is when your brain's reward system finally gets to cash the check.

When you achieve a goal, your brain releases a flood of powerful neurochemicals, and the most famous of these is dopamine. Often misunderstood as the "pleasure chemical," dopamine is more accurately the "motivation chemical." [32] Its primary role is to make you want to repeat behaviors that lead to rewards. When you complete a cycle and achieve your mission, the resulting dopamine hit is your brain's way of saying, "That was good. Pay attention to the actions that led to this result, and do them again."

When you make a point to celebrate your win, you're telling your brain to highlight a key moment so you can repeat it in the future. If you skip this step, you miss out on a powerful chance to reinforce the habits and actions that led to your success.

But it's not just about dopamine. Celebration also boosts serotonin, a neurotransmitter associated with feelings of pride, social status, and overall well-being. [33] When you acknowledge your success, especially when you share it with a trusted inner circle, your brain recognizes it as a rise in your social standing.

This boost in serotonin is a key component of what neuroscientist Ian Robertson calls the "Winner Effect." His research indicates that the act of winning can chemically alter the brain, making individuals more confident, smarter, and more willing to take on future challenges.[34] Small, celebrated wins chemically prime you for bigger wins by reconfiguring your brain's chemistry in your favor.

Finally, celebrating is a powerful antidote to the stress of the grind. The Waxing Phases are a period of high effort, high pressure, and, often, high levels of the stress hormone cortisol. Chronic exposure to high levels of cortisol is what leads to burnout.[35] The act of celebrating, and specifically the practice of "savoring," has been shown to actively reduce cortisol levels.

To get the most out of your celebration, make it specific: know exactly what you're celebrating, and make it a ritual. Celebrate as soon as possible after your win, so your brain associates the reward with the effort. Share the moment with your inner circle to boost the feeling of recognition. Make it physical, whether that's a special meal, a walk, or something else that marks the occasion. And take a moment to reflect, feeling gratitude for the journey and linking your reward to the work you put in. This isn't just about throwing a party; it's a key part of your growth.

The Operator's Mindset

Once the celebration is complete, the nature of your work undergoes a fundamental shift. The builder puts down their hammer, and the operator steps up to the control panel. Your creation is now a living, breathing entity in the world, and it requires proper management.

Being in "full execution" means you have graduated from the chaotic, heroic work of creation to the disciplined, strategic work of stewardship. This requires a completely new mindset and a new set of skills.

The Full Moon is the phase where you must force yourself to make this transition. You must stop being just a technician and start becoming a manager and a strategist. This means your primary job is no longer just to do the work, but to build the systems that allow the work to be done consistently and at scale.

You must take the heroic, ad-hoc processes you used during the Waxing Phases and turn them into documented, repeatable systems. The chef who can cook one amazing meal now needs to create a detailed recipe and a kitchen process so that their line cooks can produce one hundred amazing meals a night. This process of systematization is the core work of the operator.

As your project grows, so does its complexity. More customers, more feedback, more moving parts. The simple methods that worked in the early days won't be enough now. You need to upgrade your systems to match the new level of challenge. This means building ways to track what matters, setting up clear lines of communication, and learning how to delegate well.

Finally, the operator's mindset means recognizing that you are no longer working under the protection of a silo. When you were building in the dark, you were largely ignored. But now that you have a shining Full Moon, you are on the map, which means you have attracted the attention of competitors.

Full execution is not just about serving your current customers; it's about actively defending the hill you've just taken. You must start building a moat by maintaining a strategic advantage that makes your success difficult for others to replicate. This could be building a powerful brand that inspires deep loyalty, creating high switching costs that make it inconvenient for your customers to leave, or fostering network effects where your product becomes more valuable as more people use it.

This shift from builder to operator is one of the most difficult transitions in any ambitious journey. It requires a new level of strategic thinking and a willingness to let go of the very tasks that made you successful in the first place. This work can be broken down into three key activities: **solidifying your gains**, **embracing the feedback loop**, and **capitalizing on your momentum**.

First, you must work to **solidify your gains** and **embrace user feedback**. Now that your work is out in the world, you have access to the most valuable resource imaginable: real-world feedback. This "Full Moon" phase is about a profound shift from relying solely on internal intuition and initial assumptions to actively incorporating and responding to external data. It demands a deep sense of humility, acknowledging that your initial vision, no matter how brilliant, may not always represent the optimal path forward.

The story of Instagram exemplifies this principle perfectly.[36] The globally recognized application we use today was not the founders' original concept. It began as a highly complex, location-based social networking app called Burbn, which allowed users to check in, make plans, earn points for hanging out with friends, and post photos. When Burbn was launched, the founders meticulously observed and analyzed how users were *actually* interacting with their product. They noticed a critical pattern: while the vast majority of Burbn's features were being largely ignored or underutilized, users consistently gravitated towards and absolutely loved one specific function: the simple photo-sharing and filter feature.

In an extraordinary demonstration of strategic humility and acute market awareness, the founders made a radical decision. They didn't incrementally tweak Burbn; they ruthlessly stripped away everything that the user base wasn't using. They eliminated all the complex check-in features, the planning functionalities, and the points system, focusing exclusively on the singular feature their users demonstrably adored: photo sharing with filters.

This bold act of distillation, guided entirely by user feedback, was a pivotal moment. Their subsequent billion-dollar success, culminating in their acquisition by Facebook, was the direct result of their willingness to relentlessly iterate and pivot based on real-world feedback during their "Full Moon" phase.

This was the very definition of embracing the feedback loop, allowing overwhelming user feedback to not only inform but also drive the strategic direction of their business moving forward. It allowed them to solidify their gains, transforming their small mobile app into a globally dominant platform by giving users exactly what they wanted, even if it wasn't what the founders initially envisioned.

The third key is to **use your momentum**. The Full Moon is when your influence is at its highest, so take advantage of it to grow even more. Success attracts more success. When people see you've done well in one area, they'll be more likely to trust you in others. Use this time to build your network, strengthen your reputation, and advance your project.

It is important to remember, however, that momentum doesn't last forever. It's like catching a wave after a long wait: you're up, moving fast, and it feels amazing, but the wave will eventually break. Your job is to use that energy to get as far as you can, not just coast along. Make the most of it while it lasts; this is the moment to use your new status.

The meeting you couldn't get before is now just a call away. The investor who ignored your email is suddenly interested. People who didn't believe in you previously are now knocking down your door to get in on your next big thing. Your Full Moon is proof to the world that you're someone to watch. It silences the doubters and draws in new supporters.

Your outreach changes now. Before, you were pushing your message out, hoping someone would notice. Now, you'll feel the pull of your own success; opportunities come to you, emails land in your inbox, and people who once seemed out of reach are reaching out. The challenge isn't finding chances anymore; it's choosing the right ones to protect your time and energy. Ask yourself with every new offer: "Does this fit with my *Orbiting Ambition* and the next phase of your journey?" If it's not a clear yes, it's a no.

This is also the time to begin telling others about your story. As you may recall, one of the fundamental rules during the Waxing Phases was "show before you tell." You were in the dark, doing the unglamorous work, building your proof. Announcing your grand plans then would have been a strategic mistake; now, however, you have a tangible result and can gain more exposure by telling the story behind it.

You have the trophy, the finished product, the data. You have *shown* the world what you are capable of. Now, it is up to you to capitalize on this credibility and use it to the fullest extent possible to advance the journey towards your *Orbiting Ambition*.

The Gravity of Success

This brings us to a critical, often-overlooked aspect of the Full Moon phase. Success creates a new form of gravity. In the New Moon and Waxing Phases, you were a small object, working hard to break free from the gravitational pull of your old life and achieve a stable orbit. Now, in the Full Moon, you have become a large object yourself. Your success has created a gravitational field that begins to pull other people, opportunities, and problems into your orbit. Managing this new gravity is a crucial, high-level skill that separates those who sustain their success from those who are crushed by it.

The most immediate and tangible effect of this new gravity is the inbound flow. Your email inbox, which was once quiet, is now flooded. Your phone starts ringing with requests from people you barely know. Everyone wants a piece of your time, your expertise, or your money. If you are not careful, you will spend your entire Full Moon phase simply reacting to this inbound flow instead of being on the offensive to advance your agenda. You must build a system to manage it.

A simple but powerful framework is the "4 Ds," which is a popular time management methodology:[37]

1. **Delete:** You must become ruthless in ignoring things that are not aligned with your *Orbiting Ambition*. The vast majority of inbound requests will be distractions. Learning to say no is a strategic necessity.

2. **Delegate:** For entrepreneurs or leaders, this is about building a team and trusting them to handle tasks. For individuals, it could mean hiring a virtual assistant or even just responding with, "I'm not the right person for this, but you should talk to…" This protects your focus while still being helpful.

3. **Defer:** Not every good opportunity is a good opportunity right now. You need a system, whether it's a simple folder in your inbox or a more complex project management tool, to park interesting but non-urgent opportunities for a later date.

4. **Do:** This should be the smallest category. These are the rare opportunities that are highly aligned with your mission and require your immediate, personal attention.

At the end of the day, it's up to you to manage what comes your way. This means constantly checking in, making decisions, and protecting your most valuable resources: your time, your energy, and your focus. Think of your journey like a road trip. There are lots of roads you could take, but not all of them lead where you want to go. By using tools like the 4 Ds, you make sure you're choosing the best path and not wasting your resources on detours that won't get you closer to your goal.

Perils of the Peak: Two Shadows of the Full Moon

For all its brilliant light, the Full Moon casts the longest and darkest shadows. The peak of the mountain is the most treacherous place to be, not because the climb is hard, but because the air is thin and the fall is long. While you are busy executing your project, you must be vigilantly aware of the two great beasts that stalk every successful person and organization: **Complacency** and **Impostor Syndrome**.

The first shadow is **complacency.** If you get comfortable and stop moving forward, you risk losing everything you've worked for. Complacency is like a virus that sneaks in when you stop paying attention. Instead of using your momentum to keep growing, you let it slip away and forego your chance to keep chasing your biggest goals.

The ultimate cautionary tale in the business world is Blockbuster Video. In the late 1990s, they were a dominant, shining Full Moon. In the year 2000, they had the opportunity to buy a tiny, struggling startup called Netflix for a mere $50 million.[38] The Blockbuster executives literally laughed them out of the room. They were so blinded by the light of their own success that they were completely unable to see the future. They not only failed to buy the startup that later became their kryptonite, but they also failed to innovate beyond their traditional store model until it was too late. As we all know, within a decade, they were bankrupt, and the company no longer exists today.

The antidote to complacency is what Amazon founder Jeff Bezos calls the "Day 1" mentality.[39] It is the organizational mindset of always being a startup, of waking up every single morning with a healthy dose of concern, obsessed not with your past successes, but with your customers' current needs and the future threats on the horizon.

The second, and perhaps more insidious, shadow of the Full Moon is its psychological inverse: **Impostor Syndrome**. This is the deep, persistent, and often secret internal feeling that your success is a fraud.[40] It's the nagging voice in your head that says, "You just got lucky. Any minute now, they're going to find you out."

The cruel irony is that this feeling is most common among high achievers, like yourself. The brighter the external spotlight, the more intense the internal feeling of being a fraud can become. Your goal is to suppress the feeling of Imposter Syndrome by proving to yourself that you have earned your success.

This is part of the psychological reasoning for celebrating successes. It isn't like you've won the lottery and inherited millions of dollars; you've worked for your success, at whatever level it may be, and you deserve to be where you are.

If you spend time reflecting on your successes and align yourself with your *Orbiting Ambition*, I promise you will feel empowered and energized to continue growing your project. You may feel doubt, but you should use it as motivation to achieve even greater success.

As Frank Sinatra famously said, "the best revenge is massive success."[41] Your job is to prove all of your doubters wrong, even when your biggest doubter is yourself.

Reinvesting the Harvest: Fueling the Next Cycle

The Full Moon phase is a balancing act. You need to celebrate your success, but also guard against getting too comfortable. Use your momentum, but stay humble about the doubts that can creep in.

The smartest people know that this is the time to **reinvest**. The Full Moon is when you have extra resources, be it money, confidence, or connections. Don't just spend them, use them to plant seeds for your next round of growth.

The peak of the Full Moon is the perfect time to start thinking about your next New Moon, as you move towards the Waning Phases. Ask yourself how you can reinvest what you've gained. Start with your financial capital. Use the profits from this cycle to fund your next, bigger idea.

Then look at your social capital. With a stronger reputation and a bigger network, how can you use those connections? Maybe it's making introductions, forming new partnerships, or reaching out to a mentor for advice you couldn't have gotten before.

Finally, you must reinvest your knowledge capital. The success of your last cycle taught you invaluable lessons. How can you codify and reinvest that knowledge? This could mean creating playbooks for your team, writing a blog post to share your lessons with your industry (further building your brand), or, most powerfully, dedicating time to mentor someone else, which is the best way to solidify your own understanding.

This process of strategic reinvestment is the ultimate proactive mindset. While everyone else is admiring your harvest, you are already selecting the best seeds to plant for the next season. It is the bridge that connects the peak of the Full Moon to the productive and necessary retreat of the Waning Phase. The light of the Full Moon is brilliant, but it is not static. Anything that reaches a peak must begin a new phase. The ultimate measure of your success is not how brightly you shine at the peak, but how wisely you use that light to prepare for the next journey into the darkness.

⑨

Mastering the Full Moon
with Credibility

"Could I have been anyone other than me?"

That's the opening line to one of the greatest songs by the Dave Matthews Band called *Dancing Nancies*. If you've never heard it, do yourself a favor and listen to it in its entirety. It's incredibly reflective and inspires the kind of restless curiosity that drives the best of us to wonder: What if my life had unfolded differently?

Could I have been someone else? Maybe a banker, a poet, a stranger in a city far from here, or even just a name that faded quietly into the background?

In theory, the answer is yes. There are a thousand versions of you that could have existed. A different friend, a missed opportunity, a single moment of courage or hesitation, and your story might have unfolded in a completely new direction. Our lives are shaped by a constellation of choices and chance, each one nudging us onto a slightly different path. But beneath all those possibilities, there is a deeper truth: you are, and always have been, you.

You can change the scenery and move to a new city, take on a new title, collect new possessions, even reinvent your outward appearance. But at your core, there is something steady and unchanging, a gravitational pull that draws you toward certain interests, ideas, and ways of being. You can grow and evolve, but you can't outrun your own orbit.

This is why our reputations form around who we are at the center. Over time, that reputation becomes a kind of identity: one that can be hard to change, especially if it's not the one we want. That's why it's so important to build a reputation that is **authentic** and truly reflects your own *Orbiting Ambition*.

Consider the moon for a moment. It has a reputation for cycling through its phases, waxing and waning with a rhythm we've come to trust. We can't see the future, but we have faith that the Full Moon will return, just as it always has. The moon's consistency is so reliable that no one would bet against it. Its reputation is built on showing up, again and again.

In the same way, your reputation becomes a key part of your identity. If you are known for being inconsistent, missing commitments, or not following through, you will find that opportunities become scarce, no matter how capable you are. Your skills determine what you can do. Your reputation determines where you get the chance to do it.

Here's a truth that often goes unspoken: being good at something is only part of the equation. The world is full of talented people who never get the chance to shine, simply because no one knows what they can do. Meanwhile, others with less skill but more visibility seem to catch all the breaks. It's not just luck. It's the quiet force of reputation at work.

Think back to the last time you needed to hire someone, recommend a collaborator, or choose a partner for an important project. Did you sift through every possible option, or did you start with the names that came to mind first? Chances are, you thought of people whose reputations had already reached you. You thought of those who had shown up, delivered, and made themselves visible. That's how most decisions are made.

This is the reality: opportunities rarely go to the most qualified person in the world. They go to the most qualified person that the decision-maker knows and trusts. Your reputation is what gets you onto that short list. Without it, you are invisible. With it, doors open that you might not have even known existed.

This is why many startups tend to release their product to the public before it is truly refined (that's what we often call the "beta test" in the software world). Why do they do this? Because building something perfect in a vacuum provides no value to the outside world, and it gives competitors the chance to beat you to market.

Building visibly and releasing as soon as you have a Minimum Viable Product (MVP), however, creates visibility. While the product has to be good enough to solve the core problem for users, it doesn't have to be perfect. Once users get to see the value in the product, they tell others about it. It gains more users, more notoriety, and it establishes a reputation for being "the tool that solves this problem." Better competitors may emerge, but the reputation has already been established by the product that solved the problem first.

This chapter is about seeing your reputation as something you build with intention and care, and the Full Moon phase is when it is most vital that you establish and protect it. As Warren Buffett famously said, "It takes 20 years to build a reputation and 5 minutes to ruin it." The goal here is to help you build and keep a reputation that supports your pursuit of your *Orbiting Ambition*.

The Competence-Credibility Gap

Let me share a framework that shifted my thinking. When considering your professional value, there are two key elements that determine your marketability. The first is **competence**: this is what you can actually do, the skills you've built, and the results you can deliver. The second is **credibility**: what others believe you can do, the reputation you've earned, and the trust you've built.[42]

Early in your career, there's usually a gap where your competence exceeds your credibility. You're good at what you do, but nobody knows it yet. You can deliver results, but you don't have a proven track record to back it up. This is frustrating, but normal. Every expert was once unknown.

The real risk is getting stuck in that gap. Many people spend years, even decades, being more capable than their reputation shows. They do great work in the background, hoping someone will notice, believing that quality will speak for itself. Sometimes it does, but more often, it does not. The world is busy and crowded, and it is hard to earn attention. If you want your skills to be recognized, you have to build your credibility to match.

There is also a risk on the other side: when credibility grows faster than competence. This is the person who is great at self-promotion but cannot deliver on their promises. They might get a few chances based on reputation, but eventually, reality catches up. When that happens, their reputation can fall apart quickly and in front of everyone.

The goal is to bring these two into alignment: to build credibility that honestly reflects your competence, and to keep raising both as you grow. Your reputation should be a true signal of what you can do; not exaggerated, but not hidden either. In this chapter, we'll discuss how to build that alignment, using a familiar cyclical process.

The Three Layers of Reputation

When you think deeply about reputation, you realize that it represents far more than just one element of your character. When others talk about you on a personal level, they likely think about your personality, attitude, and reliability when talking about your reputation. They may talk about whether you are a good person, how friendly you are, and the things that you have done to help them in the past.

In professional circles, however, it is much easier to think about your reputation as the collection of traits that makes someone want to buy your services. This is where we can dive into research on sales and persuasion and discuss the elements of your reputation that most impact your marketability.

In Robert Cialdini's research, he introduced 7 Principles of Persuasion that indicate the best sales techniques that consistently work in the real world, which are reciprocity, commitment and consistency, social proof, authority, liking, scarcity, and unity.[43]

This idea is quite powerful when thinking about persuasion, since that is the ultimate goal of establishing a reputation: having it precede you and help close the deal. For our purposes, we're going to modify and adapt Cialdini's principles to focus on three that directly apply to your reputation's vitality.

I propose that your professional reputation consists of three deeply interconnected layers: **proof of work**, **social proof**, and **thought leadership**. Building all three in concert is what will create a strong, lasting reputation.

The first layer is **proof of work**. This is the tangible evidence that you can do what you claim to do. It's your portfolio, your case studies, your track record, your references. Without this foundation, everything else is smoke and mirrors. You can be the best marketer in the world, but if you have no actual work to point to, your reputation will be shallow and temporary.

Building this layer means being thoughtful about the work you choose and how you document it. Not every project will help your reputation equally. Some are visible and memorable, while others fade into the background. Some create things you can share, while others do not. Some involve people who will vouch for you, while others are just transactions.

This does not mean you should only take on high-profile work. Especially early in your journey, you should take what you can get. However, it does mean you should consider each project through the lens of reputation. Can you showcase it? Will it lead to a testimonial? Does it show a skill you want to be known for? If so, take extra care to document the details, capture the results, and get permission to share. If not, it is still worth doing, but be aware that it may not add to your reputation portfolio.

I have a friend whom I would call a "serial entrepreneur." He's started several companies, and each time he starts a new business, he goes back to the grind with one principle in mind: never turn down work. If someone calls you for something simple that may not bring in a lot of revenue, do it anyway, because you never know what that customer might have you do next if they are impressed.

They might have you do work for their company, or recommend you to their neighbors or others. They might promote your services on social media or leave you a good review. Worst case, they'll pay you to do the work, which in and of itself is a net positive for your business. If you do good work, they'll likely keep you in mind for future work.

This leads us into our second layer, **social proof.** In short, this is what others say about you. This includes testimonials, recommendations, endorsements, and referrals. Social proof is powerful because it comes from someone else. When you say you're good at something, people might doubt it. When someone else says it, people tend to believe it.

To build this layer, make it easy and natural for people to vouch for you. Most people who benefit from your work would be glad to recommend you; they just need a gentle nudge. After you've done good work, ask for their endorsement while it's still fresh in their mind. This could be a LinkedIn recommendation, a brief testimonial for your website, or even a referral to someone who needs your assistance.

A common mistake is never asking for a testimonial (maybe out of modesty or fear) or asking at the wrong time. The best time to ask is right after you've delivered value and the person is happy with the results. Make it easy for them: offer a template or a draft they can edit, instead of asking them to start from scratch. Most people want to help, as long as it's simple.

Social Proof, however, is more than just collecting testimonials. It's about building a network of people who remember you when opportunities come up. This means staying in touch, offering help without expecting anything in return, and genuinely caring about the success of others. Your reputation grows through the people who know you, trust you, and want to see you succeed.

The third layer is **thought leadership**, which is sharing your ideas and insights with others. This is where you transition from simply doing the work to demonstrating a deep understanding of your field and the ability to help others learn. Thought leadership expands your reputation, reaching people you may never meet in person.

If this sounds intimidating, remember that thought leadership does not mean you have to be a social media star or a keynote speaker. It simply means sharing what you are learning in ways that help others. This could be writing about challenges you have solved, creating tutorials, speaking at local events, or simply answering questions thoughtfully in online communities.

The key is consistency. One article or one talk will not make you a thought leader. However, sharing genuine insights regularly will help establish your reputation. Over time, as you continue to show up and provide value, you become recognized as someone who helps others grow.

These three layers — proof of work, social proof, and thought leadership — work together to create a reputation that's both authentic and powerful. Proof of work gives you legitimacy. Social proof gives you credibility. Thought leadership gives you visibility. When all three are aligned, opportunities start finding you instead of you having to chase them.

The Network Effect

Reputation isn't built in isolation. It's built through relationships, and the quality of your network determines how far your reputation can spread. This is where many highly capable people plateau: they build competence and even some credibility, but they don't invest in the relationships that would amplify their reputation beyond their immediate sphere.

Building a valuable network isn't about collecting business cards or accumulating LinkedIn connections; it's about cultivating genuine relationships with three types of people, each serving a different but essential function:

The first type is **mentors**: people who are several steps ahead of you on a path you want to walk. They've solved problems you're currently facing. They've made mistakes you can learn from. They have a perspective you lack. A good mentor doesn't just give advice; they open doors, make introductions, and vouch for you when opportunities arise. Your reputation in their eyes matters enormously because their recommendation carries weight.

Finding mentors requires being strategic about who you approach and how. The best mentors aren't necessarily the most famous people in your field, as they are often too busy and inundated with requests. The best mentors are people one or two levels above you who remember what it's like to be in your position.

Look for people whose work you genuinely admire, then find ways to provide value to them before asking for anything. Comment thoughtfully on their work. Share their articles with your network. Implement their advice and report back on results. Build a relationship based on genuine interest and mutual value.

When you do ask for mentorship, be specific about what you need. Asking "Will you be my mentor?" is too vague and too demanding, especially at first. Asking "Could I get 30 minutes of your time to discuss a specific challenge I am facing?" is more realistic and more likely to get a yes. Most successful people are happy to help; they just need to know exactly what you are asking for and why you are asking them. It is like getting a text that says "Hey" or "How are you" — you probably wish they would just get to the point and tell you what they want without wasting time with small talk.

The second type of connection you need in your network is **peers**: people at roughly your level who are working on similar challenges. These relationships are often the most valuable but also the most neglected. People often focus on networking up with mentors and influential connections, but forget to network sideways. Your peers become your community, your sounding board, your collaborators, and as you all grow, they become the network of successful people who remember when you were all starting out together.

I've observed this pattern repeatedly: individuals who invest in peer relationships early in their careers often end up with incredibly valuable networks later. The person who was a struggling entrepreneur alongside you becomes a successful founder who refers clients your way. The person who was learning to code in the same bootcamp becomes a hiring manager who brings you into a great opportunity. The person who was writing articles in obscurity alongside you becomes a well-known author who introduces you to their audience.

These relationships are built through shared struggle and mutual support. Join or create peer groups, mastermind groups, accountability circles, or just regular check-ins with people at your level. Share what you're learning, celebrate each other's successes, and support one another through challenges. These relationships aren't transactional; they're built on genuine camaraderie and reciprocal support.

The third type is **mentees**, people who are several steps behind you on the path. This might seem counterintuitive for building your network, but teaching others is one of the fastest ways to establish credibility. When you help someone else succeed, you demonstrate expertise. When they succeed and credit you, your reputation grows. The act of teaching also forces you to clarify your own thinking, which makes you better at your craft.

You do not need to be an expert to mentor someone; you just need to be a few steps ahead of them. If you are in the third year of your career, you can mentor someone in their first year. If you have completed ten Lunar Cycles mastering a skill, you can guide someone through their first cycle. The best mentors are not the ones who know everything; they are the ones who remember what it was like to know very little and can translate their knowledge into actionable guidance.

Mentoring doesn't have to be formal or time-consuming. It can be as simple as answering questions in online forums, offering feedback on someone's work, or sharing the frameworks and processes that have worked for you. Each time you do this, you build a reputation as someone who's both knowledgeable and generous: a powerful combination.

These three types of relationships create a network that amplifies your reputation in ways you can't achieve alone. Your mentors vouch for you to their networks. Your peers collaborate with you and refer opportunities to you. Your mentees credit you as they succeed. The network effect means your reputation spreads farther and grows faster than any amount of self-promotion could achieve.

But this approach only succeeds when your investment in relationships is sincere. People quickly sense the difference between genuine connection and manipulative networking. Prioritize building relationships based on a genuine interest, not just to reap benefits for yourself. Just as you can tell the difference between friends who are authentic and those who are only around for their own gain, your professional network will evaluate you based on your authenticity.

Building Reputation and Maintaining Integrity

Now, let me address the elephant in the room. For many people, deliberately building reputation feels uncomfortable, manipulative, or self-promotional. There is a cultural narrative, especially in some industries and backgrounds, that good work should speak for itself and promoting yourself is somehow unseemly. Focusing on reputation is often seen as superficial or inauthentic.

I understand this resistance because I have felt it myself. There's something that feels pure about doing excellent work in obscurity, about letting the work be enough, about not needing recognition. And there's something that feels dirty about "self-promotion" or "personal branding" or any activity that seems designed to make yourself look good.

I felt this deeply during my political campaign. As an introvert, it was incredibly difficult for me to introduce myself to strangers, share my story, and ask someone for their vote. While I was being genuine and representing a platform I truly believed in, it made me feel exhausted because it wasn't something I was used to doing. I never liked trying to talk about myself and ask others for anything, especially a vote, which I consider to be a contract between the voter and candidate to do whatever it takes to implement their platform.

While running a political campaign was exhausting and probably not something I would wish to repeat, this experience did shift my thinking about personal branding. I learned that building your reputation is not about making yourself look better than you are. It is about ensuring your actual capabilities are recognized, so you can leverage them to create value at scale. When your reputation accurately reflects your competence, you get access to bigger problems to solve, bigger projects to work on, and a bigger impact to make. Your reputation is not inflating your worth; it is revealing it.

Think about it this way: if you've genuinely solved a problem that many others face, isn't it selfish to keep that solution to yourself? If you've developed a skill that could help others succeed, isn't it a service to teach it? If you've developed capabilities that could contribute to important work, isn't it responsible to ensure the people doing that work are aware of your existence?

Reframe reputation-building from self-promotion to service. You are not trying to convince people you are better than you are. You are trying to make sure your authentic capabilities are visible so you can contribute where you are most needed. That is not manipulation; that is stewardship of your gifts.

The key to all of this is authenticity. Every piece of your credibility portfolio should be genuinely true. Every testimonial should be earned. Every thought leadership piece should provide real value. Every relationship should be built on authentic interest and reciprocity. When your reputation is built on truth, you never have to worry about being exposed as a fraud because you're not one.

As we alluded to earlier, there is also a practical reason to build your reputation ethically: reputations are hard to build and easy to destroy. One instance of inflating your achievements, one case of taking credit you did not earn, or one pattern of promising more than you can deliver is likely to spread quickly and can permanently damage your credibility. The short-term gain of overstating your capabilities is never worth the long-term cost of a damaged reputation.

Build your reputation as a true reflection of your competence, and you build something sustainable. If your reputation grows faster than your competence, you build a house of cards.

⑩

The Waning Phases

After the Full Moon reaches its brightest, the next phase arrives almost unnoticed. The moon's light doesn't vanish all at once; it gently fades, night after night. The glowing circle shrinks to a waning gibbous, then a half-moon, then a slender crescent, and finally slips into darkness, preparing for a new beginning. These are the Waning Phases.

We live in a culture that values constant progress. There's pressure to move from one achievement straight into the next, without stopping to reflect or recover. Taking a pause is often seen as a weakness or a waste of time, rather than a necessary part of growth.

We love to celebrate the big moments: the launch, the hard work, the win. We cheer for the rocket lifting off, the runner breaking the tape, the entrepreneur ringing the bell on Wall Street. These moments matter, but when we focus only on them and move straight to the next effort, we lose sight of the quiet power that comes from pausing and reflecting.

We often forget the importance of the space between efforts: the quiet moments that allow us to recover and reflect. Overlooking this need for rest is a common mistake, especially for those who are driven. It leads to burnout, causes talented people to stall, and traps many in cycles of repeating the same mistakes, working harder but not necessarily improving.

The Waning Phases aren't about losing ground, even if it feels that way when you're used to seeing progress you can measure. This is your chance to gather what you've learned, reflect on your journey, and recharge for what's ahead. It's a time to take stock, learn from your experience, and prepare for the next cycle.

People often overlook these phases, but this may be the most crucial part of the entire Lunar Cycle. When you give the Waning Phases as much attention as the planning and building stages, you set yourself up for lasting success rather than just a single win. This is how you turn one achievement into a pattern of growth, building on your learning and becoming stronger with each cycle.

A powerful analogy for this phase comes from professional sports: specifically, what happens in NFL facilities every Monday morning. While fans only see the drama of Sunday's game, the real work happens off-camera: the players spend hours in the film room, reviewing every play, seeking to find patterns, weaknesses, and opportunities for improvement.

This isn't self-criticism, it's objective analysis. The players study themselves, their teammates, and their opponents, seeking insights that will improve themselves both individually and as a team for next time. The goal is to spot and correct issues before opponents do. This quiet, behind-the-scenes analysis is where real progress happens. Mastery isn't forged under stadium lights; it's forged in the reflective work of the film room.

Most people overlook this: they focus only on the highlights, not the disciplined review that leads to growth. All the casual observers see is the fading excitement from the last big game, the highlights slowly dropping down the sports news cycle. They don't see this crucial, hidden work being done to prepare for the next game. They don't understand that the difference between a good quarterback and a great one, between a playoff team and a championship team, is not just talent or even effort, but is the quality of this reflective work and this systematic extraction of wisdom from experience.

The Waning Phases are your personal film room: a time to honestly examine your last cycle, extract lessons, and turn experience into a strategic advantage. It's not about harsh judgment, but about learning and preparing for greater success. This silent, unglamorous, deeply analytical work is what actually enables you to learn, adapt, and continuously improve. It's what allows you to show up on game day smarter, more prepared, and as a more effective leader.

This isn't the moment to be harsh with yourself or get stuck on what went wrong. Instead, use these phases to look honestly at your recent experience and turn what you've learned into a real advantage for your next cycle. This is where setbacks become wisdom, failures become knowledge, and successes become habits you can build on.

The After-Action Review: Military Precision for Personal Growth

Reflection is valuable, but without structure, it can go wrong. This often fails in two ways: it becomes either a jumble of random thoughts with no clear takeaways or a spiral of harsh self-criticism that offers no path to improvement.

To avoid both these traps, we can borrow a simple but profoundly powerful tool from one of the most effective learning organizations in the world: the United States military. It's called the **After-Action Review (AAR)**, and it has been refined over decades of high-stakes operations where the quality of learning can literally mean the difference between life and death.[44]

After every mission, every training exercise, and every significant operation, teams gather to deconstruct their experience in a structured, blame-free environment. The AAR is not a performance review where someone gets punished. It's not a platform for finger-pointing or excuse-making. It is a sacred space where the only goal is to learn as quickly and efficiently as possible from what just happened. The only currency that matters is truth and learning.

This is your system for watching your own game tape, for conducting your personal review during the Waning Phases. The AAR process revolves around four deceptively simple questions that, when answered honestly and systematically, will unlock more wisdom than a dozen self-help books.

Question 1: What Did We Set Out to Do?

Before you can evaluate your performance and assess whether you succeeded or failed, you must first establish an objective baseline. What was the plan? What were you actually trying to accomplish? This is why the One-Page Mission Roadmap you created during your New Moon phase is so critical. It becomes your source of truth, the original record of what you committed to.

Take it out now and look at it. What were your exact, written, SMART goals? What was the specific outcome you were aiming for? What were the daily or weekly actions you committed to executing?

What timeline did you set? What resources did you allocate? What assumptions did you make about how things would unfold?

This step is essential because our memories are notoriously unreliable, and they become even more unreliable when our egos are involved.

After a successful cycle, we tend to engage in revisionist history, unconsciously editing our memories to make our original plan seem more brilliant, more visionary, more inevitable than it actually was. "I always knew this would work" becomes the rewritten narrative, even if your artifacts from the New Moon phase reveal that you were terrified and uncertain.

After a failure, we do the opposite: we downplay our original ambitions to soften the psychological blow and to protect our self-image. "I wasn't really trying that hard anyway" or "I knew it was a long shot" becomes the protective story we tell ourselves, even if the evidence shows we were fully committed.

The One-Page Mission Roadmap serves as your defense against both forms of self-deception. It is the documented plan, written before you knew how things would turn out, before success or failure could color your memory. It is your objective baseline, the standard against which you will measure your actual results. Treat it as your source of truth, especially when that truth is uncomfortable.

Question 2: What Actually Happened?

This is where you must become a ruthless, dispassionate journalist. Your only task at this stage is to collect the raw, uninterpreted data of the cycle, without any justification or storytelling. Just collect and state the facts.

What were the final numbers? If you had a revenue target, what was the actual revenue? If you had a goal to publish twelve blog posts, how many did you actually publish? If you committed to working out four times per week, what was your actual average? What was the timeline from start to finish? How long did it actually take, and what was the cost?

What was the specific, unfiltered feedback you received from the people who interacted with your work? What did clients actually say in their reviews, not what you remember them saying or what you wish they had said? What did your metrics show? Not the vanity metrics you can spin positively, but the core metrics that actually matter? How many people saw your work? How many took action? How many came back?

You must resist the powerful urge to tell a story or make excuses at this stage. Right now, you're just establishing what is objectively, verifiably true. You hit your sales target, or you missed it by 20%. The project either took three weeks or it took five weeks. The client was either happy or unsatisfied.

Laying out this objective data first, before you allow yourself to interpret it, prevents the review from becoming a session of feelings-based speculation or motivated reasoning. It anchors you in reality. It provides a solid foundation for analysis in the next step.

Question 3: Why Did It Happen?

Now, and only now, can you begin your analysis. Your task in this third question is to explore the gap between your plan from Question 1 and your results from Question 2. This is where the real learning occurs, where experience is transformed into wisdom. With that being said, it is absolutely crucial that you analyze your successes with the same rigor and skepticism that you apply to your failures.

This is the mistake most people make. They obsess over their failures, picking them apart endlessly, but they gloss over their wins. When something goes well, they often attribute it to generic explanations: "We worked hard," "The team really pulled together," or even just "We got lucky." Then they move on, learning almost nothing from their success, which means they have no idea how to replicate it.

This is a catastrophic missed opportunity. You must deconstruct your successes with precision. When something worked better than expected, you need to understand exactly why. You must drill down until you find the specific, replicable factors that led to the positive outcome.

The reasoning behind this extensive investigation is straightforward: if you can identify what actually works, you can do more of it deliberately rather than hoping to stumble into success again. You can turn lucky accidents into strategic advantages, and you can build systems around the things that worked in the next Lunar Cycle.

The same approach must be applied to your failures and shortfalls. Take a specific goal you missed or a thing that went wrong. Don't just acknowledge that it didn't work; try to uncover the reasons why it failed.

The goal in this analysis is not to assign blame to yourself or anyone else. Blame is useless; it's an emotional reaction that prevents learning. The goal is to uncover the systemic flaws, the specific decisions, and the hidden assumptions that led to the results you got. When you identify those factors clearly, you create the possibility of changing them.

Question 4: What Will We Do Differently Next Time?

The final question of the AAR is what transforms the entire exercise into a high-performance tool. The primary purpose of this review is not only to understand the past, but also to do so in order to shape the future. The output of your AAR should not be a vague sense of "lessons learned" that you'll probably forget in a week, but rather reflect an actionable list of specific changes you will implement in your next cycle.

You can organize this into 3 different groups: things you keep doing, things you should stop doing, and things you should start doing.

Keep Doing: Based on your analysis, what are the specific things you will continue doing because they were highly effective? Be specific and include details that explain why these things are effective.

Stop Doing: What are the specific things you will stop doing because they were ineffective, inefficient, or actively harmful? Think of the time-wasters, the strategies that sound good but don't work, and the habits that drain energy without producing results.

Start Doing: What are the specific new things you will begin implementing in your next cycle based on what you learned? These are your experiments, your adaptations, and the concrete changes you're making in response to the data.

This list becomes one of the most valuable inputs for your next New Moon phase. It ensures that your learning is not just a theoretical exercise, but immediately becomes an actionable strategy that makes your next cycle demonstrably more effective than the last one. This is how you compound your learning across cycles, and how you get exponentially better each time.

Creating a Culture of Learning

This process of systematic, ruthless, ego-free review is the engine that powers all truly high-performance organizations. It's what separates the companies that dominate their industries for decades from the ones that have one good year and then fade into irrelevance. It's the difference between individuals who plateau after an initial success and those who continue growing throughout their entire careers.

Consider Ray Dalio, the founder of Bridgewater Associates, one of the world's largest and most successful hedge funds. Dalio has built his entire organization on a culture of what he calls "radical transparency." [45] At Bridgewater, every mistake, from the smallest error in a financial model to major strategic miscalculations, is meticulously documented and analyzed in a company-wide "issue log." [46]

This isn't intended to punish anyone or to create a fear of making mistakes. In fact, failing to document and learn from mistakes is a much more serious offense than making them in the first place. The cultural expectation at Bridgewater is that every error, every failed hypothesis, and every wrong prediction becomes an opportunity for the entire organization to learn. The goal is to create a system where the same mistake is literally never made twice, not by the same person, and not by anyone else in the organization, because the learning is captured and shared.

This might seem extreme or even oppressive to people accustomed to corporate cultures where mistakes are hidden, blamed on others, or quietly swept under the rug. But it is a testament to the extraordinary power of institutionalizing the Waning Phases. It's what allows Bridgewater to continuously adapt, maintain exceptional performance across decades, and compound its learning at the organizational level rather than relying on individual genius.

Dalio expands on these principles in his bestselling book *Principles*, which is a 600-page codification of his life's lessons. He attributes Bridgewater's sustained success not to having smarter people or better technology, but to having better systems for extracting wisdom from experience. They've built the idea of the Waning Phases into their DNA, making organizational learning as systematic and reliable as their investment algorithms.

You can do the same thing at the individual level. Even if you're not running a hedge fund, even if you're just trying to build a side business, advance your career, or write a book, you can build this discipline into your personal operating system. You can create your own issue log and learning repository. Every cycle, every project, and every significant effort becomes an opportunity to become smarter, refine your approach, and build advantages that compound over time.

This is what separates the people who achieve one success and then struggle to replicate it from the people who build careers of serial achievement. The first group treats each success as a stroke of luck. The second group treats each success as a data point in an ongoing experiment, a lesson to be extracted and applied to the next challenge.

The Deliberate Recharge

After you have completed the hard, analytical work of your After-Action Review, there is one final, absolutely essential task you must complete before you can even think about your next New Moon: **you must deliberately and intentionally recharge**.

This is not optional. This is not something you do if you happen to have extra time. This is a strategic necessity, as important as any planning or execution work you do. In our "hustle culture," our addiction to productivity and our obsession with being busy often lead us to view rest as a sign of laziness, weakness, or a lack of commitment. This is not only wrong, but also dangerously misguided.

The single biggest threat to any long-term ambitious vision is not a lack of talent, a lack of strategy, or insufficient effort. It is burnout. And burnout is not just feeling tired or having a bad week. Burnout is a state of chronic emotional, physical, and mental exhaustion that fundamentally compromises your ability to function. It can take months or even years to fully recover from. It destroys careers, relationships, health, and dreams; however, it is entirely preventable through proper management of your energy cycles.

High performance is not about working harder or longer. Working yourself into the ground is not a badge of honor; it's a strategic error. The smartest, most effective performers in every field, from business to athletics to the arts, understand that rest is not the opposite of work. Rest is an integral part of work. It's not something you do despite your ambitions; it's something you do in service of your ambitions.

This isn't motivational rhetoric. This is biology. During periods of rest, your body and mind don't just passively "do nothing." They actively recover, consolidate learning, and prepare for the next round of effort. Elite athletes understand this viscerally. Muscle is not built during the workout, when you're lifting weights and tearing muscle fibers; it is built during the recovery period afterward, when your body repairs and strengthens those fibers in anticipation of future stress. Your mind, creativity, willpower, and decision-making capacity all operate on the same principle.

When you don't allow adequate recovery, you're not just tired; you're actively degrading your capacity. Your decision-making becomes impaired, your creativity wanes, your emotional regulation fails, your immune system weakens, and your relationships suffer because you have no energy left to invest in them. The work you produce is of lower quality, taking you longer to achieve worse results. You enter a death spiral where you're working harder and harder to achieve less and less, until eventually something breaks, be it your health, your mind, a crucial relationship, or the project itself.

The Waning Phases are your systematic defense against this entirely preventable catastrophe. It's when you deliberately refill the tanks you've been running on empty.

Active Rest: The Four Dimensions of Recovery

It is crucial, however, to distinguish between passive rest and active rest, because they produce dramatically different outcomes. Passive rest is the default for most people. It's collapsing on the couch after a hard week and numbing out with a few hours of Netflix. It's mindlessly scrolling through social media, watching other people's lives instead of living your own. It's having a few beers to "unwind," which actually disrupts your sleep and leaves you more tired.

While this kind of passive consumption can feel like a break in the moment, it often leaves you feeling more lethargic, more drained, and more disconnected than when you started. You're not recharging; you're just avoiding. Active rest, on the other hand, is the intentional choice of activities that specifically replenish your depleted energy reserves. It requires more initial effort, but it produces genuine recovery rather than temporary escape.

Think of your energy as having four key, interconnected dimensions: **physical**, **mental**, **social**, and **creative**.[47] The Waning Phases are your opportunity to intentionally refuel each one:

Physical Energy is the most obvious dimension, and yet it's the one most commonly neglected by ambitious people who see their bodies as inconvenient vessels for their brains. Your physical energy is replenished through three non-negotiable pillars: sleep, nutrition, and movement.

Sleep is not a luxury or a sign of laziness; it's when your brain consolidates memories, clears metabolic waste, and resets your emotional regulation systems. Chronic sleep deprivation impairs your cognitive function to a degree equivalent to being legally drunk.[48] Would you make important business decisions drunk? Of course not. Yet people routinely make critical decisions on four or five hours of sleep, wondering why their judgment seems off.

Nutrition is fuel, plain and simple. It's easy to get off track during intense work periods, and I know this from experience. There are many times I've defaulted to fast food when I should've been eating a salad, grabbed another coffee when I needed water, or skipped meals entirely because I was "too busy."

In the moment, these choices feel efficient, since you're saving time and staying focused. But you're borrowing energy from tomorrow to fuel today, and the debt compounds with costly interest. During your Waning Phases, if you've let nutrition slip, the remedy is straightforward: get back on track before your next New Moon begins. Cook real meals. Eat vegetables. Drink water. Treat your body like the high-performance machine it is, rather than as a garbage disposal.

Movement is equally non-negotiable. You don't have to become an athlete, but you need to move your body regularly. Physical activity increases blood flow to your brain, releases endorphins that improve mood, and quite literally changes your brain chemistry in ways that enhance cognitive function and emotional resilience.[49] A thirty-minute walk does more for your mental clarity than another hour of "thinking really hard" at your desk.

Mental Energy is your capacity for focus, analysis, decision-making, and complex problem-solving. The intense cognitive demands of the Waxing and Full Moon phases significantly deplete this resource. If you move directly from one intensive cycle into another without recovery, you're operating with a cognitive deficit that compounds over time.

Mental rest is about giving your analytical, executive-function brain a complete break. This doesn't mean doing nothing, as that often makes anxious achievers more anxious. Instead, it means engaging in activities that use a different part of your brain: activities that don't require strategic thinking or decision-making.

This could mean practicing meditation or mindfulness, which trains your attention without demanding cognitive output. It could mean going for long walks in nature without your phone, letting your mind wander without trying to solve anything. It could mean engaging in simple, manual hobbies like gardening or cooking that require presence and attention but don't tax your strategic thinking centers.

For me personally, mental recovery happens most effectively on the golf course. For four hours, I'm away from all screens, immersed in nature, focused on a specific physical challenge that requires concentration but not strategic planning about my work. The complexity of golf engages my mind fully, but in a completely different mode than business thinking. I return from those sessions with my mental clarity restored in ways that no amount of "trying to relax" at home ever achieves.

The key is finding activities that are absorbing enough to keep you present but different enough from your work to allow genuine recovery. What you're looking for is not just distraction, but restoration through activities that rebuild your capacity for focus rather than just avoiding the need for it.

Social Energy is perhaps the most misunderstood dimension because people assume it's binary: you're either an introvert who needs solitude or an extrovert who needs people. In reality, everyone needs both, just in different ratios and at different times. What matters is recognizing what you need and intentionally creating it.

Depending on your mission and personality, you may have spent the last cycle in intense collaboration with others. If so, your social energy is likely depleted, and you need to engage in deliberate solitude. This means taking a break from draining social obligations, saying no to networking events, and skipping the parties where you have to "be on." It means spending time alone or with just one or two people with whom you can simply "be."

Conversely, if your last cycle involved deep, isolated work, such as writing alone, coding alone, or working on a solo project, you may have plenty of solitude energy but be starving for genuine human connection. In that case, your Waning Phases should involve reconnecting with friends, family, and your community. Not shallow networking, not transactional relationships, but forging real connections with people who matter to you.

Whether you're an introvert, an extrovert, or somewhere in between, you need to identify what actually energizes you socially and intentionally work toward recharging those batteries during this phase. Maybe it's going to a concert where you're surrounded by people but not required to interact. Maybe it's hosting a dinner party for close friends where the conversation is genuine and relaxed. Maybe it's volunteering for a cause you care about, finding meaning in service. Perhaps it's simply having coffee with a friend and discussing life instead of work.

The goal is authentic social engagement in whatever form restores you, not the performative socializing that drains you further while pretending to connect.

Creative Energy is the final dimension, and it's the one most commonly overlooked by people in analytical or operational fields who don't consider themselves "creative." Although some of us are more analytical than artistic, creativity is not exclusive to artists. It represents your ability to see new possibilities, make unexpected connections, and solve problems in novel ways. It's what allows you to innovate rather than just optimize. And it's a well that can run completely dry if you never refill it.

Your creativity is not a pipeline with an endless supply. It's a well that must be consciously replenished by consuming beautiful, interesting, inspiring things. This could mean visiting a museum and letting yourself be moved by art, even if you don't understand it intellectually. It could mean listening to a great album from start to finish; not as background noise while you work, but as the sole focus of your attention. It could mean reading a novel in a genre you've never explored, letting yourself be transported into a completely different world. It could mean watching a thunderstorm roll in, observing the raw power and beauty of nature.

Personally, I find creative recharge through painting and writing. These activities force me to see the world differently: to notice light, composition, color, and movement. They engage my creative brain, the part that sees possibilities rather than problems. When I return to my work after these creative sessions, I bring fresh perspectives that would never emerge from just "thinking harder" about business challenges.

The key is that creative recharge should be used to recharge you, not to engage in more productivity. You're not creating with the intention of producing something marketable; you're creating to rest and recharge your creative muscles. There's no deadline, no deliverable, no one to impress. You're just engaging with a world of open possibilities instead of trying to solve the world's problems. And by doing so, you're solving your own problems and refilling your reservoir of creative spirit.

The Bridge to Renewal

As your Waning Phases draw to a close, as you feel your energy reserves refilled and your mind clear from the rest and reflection, you'll begin to feel a form of restlessness appear that lets you know you are ready for your next New Moon. Your mind, rested and informed by everything you've learned, will naturally begin generating new possibilities, new questions, new visions of what "could be."

This is the signal that you're ready to transition back into a New Moon phase. Not because someone is pressuring you, not because you "should" be productive, but because you're genuinely ready; physically recovered, mentally clear, emotionally recharged, and creatively inspired. You have harvested the wisdom from your last cycle. You have identified what to keep, what to stop, and what to start. You have refilled your tanks. You have, perhaps, even discovered the need for a pivot that will fundamentally change your trajectory.

The darkness of the New Moon no longer feels threatening. It feels full of potential and possibility. You're not running from the exhaustion of your last cycle into a desperate new attempt; you're stepping confidently into the next phase of growth, armed with everything you've learned, rested and ready, prepared to build something even better than what came before.

This is the gift of the Waning Phases: this bridge between accomplishment and aspiration, between what was and what could be. It honors both the effort you've invested and the potential that still lies ahead. It ensures that your ambition remains sustainable and that your growth continues across decades, rather than peaking and then crashing. It's what allows you to chase your *Orbiting Ambition* beyond a set of predefined goals.

The next New Moon awaits, and this time, you don't enter it as the same person who began the last cycle. You enter it wiser, stronger, more capable. You enter it with systems that work, with knowledge hard-won, with capacity restored. You enter it ready not just to repeat your last success, but to transcend it.

(11)

When Reflection Reveals Revolution

Most of the time, the wisdom you gain from your review during the Waning Phases is incremental. You might identify small adjustments or optimizations that make your next cycle a little easier. Perhaps you discover a more effective approach, realize you work best at certain times of day, or notice a skill you want to develop. These small improvements, when compounded over many cycles, are powerful. They are how you move from good to great, and from competent to masterful.

But every so often, your reflection reveals something much deeper. It may show you that the entire mission you just completed, even if you technically succeeded, was aimed at the wrong target. In these moments, the most valuable outcome is not the achievement itself, but the realization that you need to make a significant, and sometimes daunting, change in direction.

This is the essence of a pivot, and the Waning Phases are where these insights are born. In the quiet space of reflection, away from the pressure of constant action, you gain the perspective to see whether you have been climbing the right mountain after all.

Two Legendary Pivots: YouTube and Slack

Consider the story of what is now one of the most dominant platforms on the internet, a site so ubiquitous that its name has become a verb: YouTube. This website now has a profound influence on culture, launches careers, and impacts billions of people. But YouTube did not start as the video-sharing colossus we know today. It began with a completely different vision, one that failed so thoroughly that most people are unaware it even existed. While I'll include the highlights here, this was covered extensively in an episode of Acquired, and I highly recommend you listen to this podcast episode if you're interested in learning more.[50]

The original concept was a video dating site with the tagline "Tune In, Hook Up." The founders' hypothesis was straightforward: online dating was exploding, and they believed people would want to upload short videos of themselves to attract romantic partners. It seemed logical; video would let people showcase their personality better than static photos and text. They built the technology, launched the site, and waited for users to flood in. The only problem was, they didn't.

Their first Full Moon was a failed launch. Hardly anyone used the site for its intended purpose. The dating concept was dead on arrival. But instead of simply declaring failure and moving on, the founders did something that separated them from the countless entrepreneurs who fail and quit: they went into their Waning Phases with honest eyes. They conducted a thorough After-Action Review of their user activity, analyzing the behavior of the limited traffic they had.

What they discovered was fascinating. While essentially nobody wanted to upload videos of themselves for the specific purpose of dating, a few curious users were ignoring the dating premise entirely and simply using the platform to share random videos, such as funny home clips, vacation footage, or short films. These users loved the underlying technology, as the ability to upload and share videos easily and freely was rare in 2005; they just didn't have any interest in using the platform for dating.

The learning was profound and uncomfortable: the dating concept, the thing they'd built the entire company around, was a complete failure. But the core technology, the video infrastructure they'd developed, was potentially powerful. They just needed the right application for it.

They made the courageous decision to pivot completely. They abandoned their original idea entirely, stripped away all the dating features and positioning, and relaunched with a radically simple premise: "Broadcast Yourself." No matchmaking, no profiles, no romantic intent. Just pure video sharing, where anyone could upload almost anything and share it with the world.

That pivot is the reason you can now watch any video you can imagine, anytime you want, on any topic, from creators all over the world. Google acquired YouTube for $1.65 billion just 18 months after the pivot. Today, it's worth well over $100 billion and is the second-most-visited website on Earth.[50/51]

A remarkably similar story played out with Slack, the workplace communication tool that has fundamentally changed how millions of teams collaborate. Slack was not originally trying to revolutionize business communication. The company was trying to build something completely different: a quirky, non-combat-based online video game called Glitch. Once again, this story is covered deeply on an episode of *How I Built This*, in which these details are based.[52]

For years, the founders of Glitch poured their energy and millions of dollars of investor money into this game. They hired talented developers, created whimsical art, and designed intricate game mechanics. They believed deeply in their vision. The game launched in 2011 with significant media attention, but unfortunately, it failed. Despite the quality of the work, the creativity, and the effort, the game never gained the traction it needed to be economically viable. By 2012, it was clear the game would have to shut down.

As the company was on the verge of collapse, with preparations underway to lay off employees and return what little money they had left to investors, founder Stewart Butterfield and his team conducted what could have been their final After-Action Review. Before walking away entirely, they asked themselves a crucial question: was there anything from this failure worth salvaging?

As they deconstructed the wreckage of Glitch, they realized that the most valuable thing they had created wasn't the game itself. It was an internal chat tool they had built for their own developers to communicate and collaborate more efficiently while building the game. Born of their own frustration with email and existing chat tools, they'd created something that was fast, searchable, organized into channels, integrated with other tools, and just fundamentally better than anything else available.

They'd built it for themselves, for their own internal need, without thinking of it as a product. But as they reviewed the failure of their game, they recognized they'd accidentally built something extraordinary. This realization led to a massive, gut-wrenching pivot.

They killed the game entirely, bet everything on this internal tool, polished it, and released it to the world as Slack.

That tool went on to become one of the fastest-growing business applications in history. It reached a $1 billion valuation faster than any software company before it. Salesforce eventually acquired it for $27.7 billion in 2021.[53] The team that built a failed video game went on to redefine workplace communication as we knew it.

These stories are powerful not just because they showcase successful companies, but because they illustrate the ultimate potential of the Waning Phases conducted with courage and honesty. The review process is not just about optimizing your current path. It's about having the wisdom and courage to realize if you're on the wrong path entirely, and the conviction to change direction even when it means abandoning work you've already invested in.

Sometimes, the most valuable outcome of a cycle is the difficult lesson that leads you to a more meaningful and aligned mission. But you only gain this insight if you are willing to ask yourself the hard questions and face the answers honestly. The Waning Phases are not just a formality or a box to check: they are a space for truth and clarity.

The Signal vs. The Noise

First, it's important to clarify what it truly means to pivot. Pivoting is not the same as giving up at the first sign of difficulty. It is not about quitting because things have become challenging, or because you're tired, or because you've had a rough week. That is not a pivot; that is simply walking away.

A pivot is a fundamental change in direction based on real data you've learned about your journey so far. It's what happens when your reflection during the Waning Phases reveals that the core assumptions underlying your mission were wrong, and no amount of tactical adjustment will fix it.

The challenge is distinguishing between the two. How do you know if you're facing normal turbulence that requires persistence, or fundamental misalignment that requires a pivot?

I like to look at 3 core signals that can indicate if the mission is still worth pursuing as-is:

Signal 1: The Motivation Has Died

Remember the Ignition Test from your New Moon phase? When you read your mission statement, did you feel that spark of excitement? Now, several cycles in, read it again. How does it feel?

If you feel nothing, not just tired, but genuinely apathetic, that's a signal. If thinking about continuing this path feels heavy and obligatory rather than energizing, something fundamental is wrong.

The key distinction: Temporary exhaustion feels like "I need a break." Fundamental misalignment feels like "I don't care anymore, and no amount of rest is going to change that."

Signal 2: You're Getting Better but Not Happier

You're objectively improving, your skills are growing, and your metrics are trending up; the work is getting easier, but it's less interesting. You should be enjoying it more, but instead, you're enjoying it less.

I've seen this with people who thought they wanted to be managers. They work their way up. They get good at management. And they discover they absolutely hate managing people. They miss doing the technical work, they resent the politics, and they find the meetings draining. They've achieved success, but they're successful at the wrong thing.

The key distinction: Normal struggle feels like "This is hard, but I'm glad I'm doing it." Fundamental misalignment feels like "I'm succeeding at something I don't actually want."

Signal 3: Your Best Self Isn't Showing Up

In your reflections during the Waning Phases, look honestly at who you became during this cycle. Are you proud of that person? Did you show up with integrity, energy, and creativity? Or did you find yourself cutting corners, avoiding hard conversations, doing work you're not proud of?

When you're aligned with your *Orbiting Ambition*, even difficult work tends to bring out your best qualities. When you're misaligned, even simple tasks tend to bring out compromised versions of yourself.

The key distinction: Temporary moral fatigue is normal and can be alleviated with rest. Persistent moral compromise is a sign you're on the wrong path.

The Pivot Decision Framework

If you have identified several pivot signals, the next question is: what should you pivot toward? And how do you decide whether to change direction or continue on your current path? Here's a systematic process to help you sort out your pivot plan:

Step 1: Separate the Mission from the Method

Often, it is not your *Orbiting Ambition* that needs to change, but rather your current approach to pursuing it.

Write down two things:

1. Your *Orbiting Ambition*
2. Your current mission

Now ask yourself: Is the challenge I'm facing with my purpose, or with the path I am taking to reach it?

Example: Maybe your *Orbiting Ambition* is "help people build financial security." Your current mission is "build a financial planning practice." After three cycles, you're discovering you hate the administrative work, the sales aspect drains you, and you're not good at client management.

The question is: Do you hate helping people with finances? Or do you hate running a financial planning practice?

If it is the latter, you **do not** need to abandon your *Orbiting Ambition*; you may simply need to change your method. Perhaps you write about personal finance, build helpful tools, or teach financial literacy in schools. The purpose remains; the approach evolves.

However, if you've realized that you actually don't care about financial security at all and you were just chasing it because it seemed lucrative or prestigious, that's a deeper problem requiring a more significant pivot. In this case, go back to Chapter 1 and work through the exercises to discover your true *Orbiting Ambition*.

Step 2: The Sunk Cost Audit

It is human nature to struggle with the idea of sunk costs. When we have invested time, energy, and even our sense of self into something, walking away can feel like admitting that the investment was wasted.

Here's the brutal truth: the investment is already gone. You can't get it back, whether you continue or quit. The only question is: what's the best use of your **future** time?

Imagine someone offered you $5,000 to quit this mission right now and do something else. Would you take it, or would you turn it down because you genuinely want to keep going?

If you'd take the money instantly and feel relieved, you already know this isn't the right path. You're only continuing because of sunk costs, fear of judgment, or inability to admit you made a mistake.

If you'd turn down the money because you genuinely believe in what you're building and just need to solve some problems, that's different. That's not a pivot signal; that's a tactical challenge.

Step 3: The Regret Minimization Framework

Jeff Bezos used this when deciding whether to leave his stable job to start Amazon. He called it the Regret Minimization Framework.[54]

Project yourself to age 80. Look back at this moment. Which choice will you regret more:

1. Continuing on this path, investing more years, and possibly discovering later that it was wrong.

2. Pivoting now, accepting the sunk costs, and pursuing something more aligned.

Most people discover that at the end of their life, they'll regret the years wasted on the wrong path, not the "failure" of admitting a mistake and changing direction early.

This only works, however, if you are honest with yourself. If you use this as an excuse to walk away from something that simply feels hard, your future self may regret not persevering. The question is not, "Which feels more comfortable right now?" but rather, "Which choice serves my *Orbiting Ambition* best?"

Step 4: The Opportunity Cost Calculation

Every hour you spend on your current mission is an hour you can't spend on something else. What are you choosing not to do because you're committed to this?

Make two lists:

- **List 1:** What I'm currently pursuing (be specific)
- **List 2:** What I would pursue if this option disappeared (be equally specific)

Now, compare these lists honestly. Which one excites you more? Which one better serves your deeper ambition? Which one draws on your true strengths?

If the second list consistently feels more inspiring than the first, you may have found your answer.

Step 5: The Small Bet Test

Before making a full pivot, can you test the alternative with a small bet?

Perhaps you're considering a transition from corporate work to starting your own business. Before quitting your job, can you spend three months building something on the side? Can you take a sabbatical? Can you undertake a small consulting project to determine if you genuinely enjoy the work?

A pivot may still be necessary, but approaching it as a thoughtful experiment, rather than an all-or-nothing leap, can reduce risk and provide clearer insight.

Of course, there are times when a small experiment is not possible, and you must commit fully to discover if something will work. In those moments, it is important to accept that reality before you move forward.

Ultimately, the work of the Waning Phases requires significant courage, whether the results reveal the need to make minor adjustments or to pivot completely. You have to decide if your current trajectory is or isn't aligned with your *Orbiting Ambition*, and only you can make this decision. Remember that the *Lunar Phase Framework* is cyclical for a reason; it isn't intended for you to reach your *Orbiting Ambition* in one cycle. The intent is to continuously review and adjust as needed. As long as you are honest with yourself and chase what you truly believe in, you will arrive at destinations you could have never imagined.

Taking the Moonshot

Now that you've completed a full Lunar Cycle, identified your *Orbiting Ambition* and charted a course towards it, you may find yourself standing at the edge of something even greater. This is the moment to consider taking a step beyond anything you've attempted before: your own Moonshot.

You've likely heard the word 'moonshot' used in all sorts of settings, often as shorthand for bold or ambitious projects. But if we look back, the term comes from a very real, audacious goal: the United States' commitment in the 1960s to land a person on the moon and bring them safely home.

Although today we live in an era where space travel seems to occur almost routinely, it is important to remember how monumental this goal was at the time. President Kennedy's vision to reach the moon before the Soviet Union was unprecedented, and the challenge itself was unlike anything the world had seen. This moonshot was not just ambitious; it was defined by three qualities that set it apart from any previous goal:

1. **It was technically possible but practically uncertain.** The physics of getting to the moon weren't science fiction; they were known. But whether we could actually execute it safely, and before anyone else, was unknown.

2. **It required becoming something we'd never been before.** America wasn't a space-faring nation when Kennedy made that commitment. We lacked the necessary technology, expertise, and infrastructure. The moonshot forced us to develop everything. We

couldn't achieve the goal by being who we already were; we had to evolve.

3. **It had a clear outcome.** Either we'd land on the moon by the deadline or we wouldn't. There was no partial credit. This meant every decision, every allocation of resources, every technical solution was measured against a singular, unambiguous standard: does this get us closer to landing on the moon?

In the same way, your own Moonshot should carry these qualities. It should be something that, **while technically within reach**, **still feels uncertain** in practice. You may not know for sure whether you can accomplish it, but you also cannot say with certainty that it is out of reach.

A true Moonshot also asks you to **grow into someone you have not yet become**. If you could achieve this goal simply by remaining as you are now, it would not be a Moonshot; it would simply be a large goal. The essence of a Moonshot is that it calls for transformation.

Clarity is also essential. While your Moonshot may not have a single, binary outcome like the original moon landing, **it should be defined clearly enough that you will know, without question, whether you have reached it**. For example, "become successful" is too vague to guide you, but "build an e-commerce company that reaches $10,000 in monthly revenue" is specific. Once again, specific goals provide the kind of clarity that fuels real progress.

This distinction is important because clarity directs your energy and focus. When your target is vague, it becomes easy to move the goalposts or to settle for less than you intended. When your goal is clear, you are able to measure your progress honestly, and you are called to face the reality of your efforts rather than negotiate with yourself.

The 3 Fears of Moonshots

Moonshots require intense levels of commitment and risk. They aren't your typical goals that you may chase on the side; they're beyond anything you've ever attempted previously. Because of this, it is reasonable to fear and avoid taking moonshots for a variety of reasons; however, if you give in to fear and choose to walk away, you'll never know if you could've landed on the moon.

In most cases, there are 3 types of fear that plague those considering a moonshot: the fear of failure, the fear of success, and the fear of permanence. Let's explore each of these in detail so that you can learn to identify and conquer them as they arise.

Fear of Failure: The Comfortable Prison

The fear of failure is the most socially acceptable fear. Everyone understands it. Everyone's felt it. It's the voice that says, "What if you try and it doesn't work? What if you invest all this time and energy and come up short? What if people watch you fail publicly? What if you discover you're not as capable as you thought?"

This fear feels rational because failure is, in fact, a possibility. Your Moonshot might not work. You might fall short. You might face embarrassment, financial loss, wasted time, or the confirmation of your deepest insecurities. Yet, what the fear of failure often hides is that remaining where you are, instead of chasing your Moonshot, can also be a form of failure.

The person who never attempts their Moonshot because they're afraid of failing has already failed. They've failed to honor their own potential, failed to take themselves seriously, and failed to give their gifts to the world. However, because this failure occurs privately, in the space between "what is" and "what could be," it doesn't register as a failure. It just registers as "being realistic," or "waiting for the right time."

The comfort of not trying can feel safe, precisely because it shields you from judgment. Dreams that remain unspoken cannot be criticized, and efforts never attempted cannot be questioned. Setbacks that never occur remain invisible.

But deep down, you are aware. You sense when you are holding yourself back, allowing fear to guide your choices. You notice the passage of time, and you may feel the distance growing between who you are and who you could become.

Here's the reframe that changed everything for me: I'm going to fail at something no matter what. The only question is what kind of failure I want to live with.

Do I want the failure that comes from trying and falling short: the kind of failure that teaches, that builds character, that at least gives me the dignity of knowing I had the courage to step into the ring?

Or, do I want the failure that comes from never trying: the kind that slowly morphs into regret? Do I want the kind of failure that whispers "what if" during every quiet moment, and that turns into bitterness toward people who had the courage I lacked?

When you look at it from this perspective, the choice becomes clearer. You can risk failing in the pursuit of your Moonshot, learning and growing along the way, or you can risk missing out on the life you are capable of living. The first kind of failure is temporary and can be overcome; the second lingers much longer.

Fear of Success: The Invisible Cage

The fear of success may sound like a paradox. We don't talk about it because, in most cases, we feel that success is the goal; however, it is often the case that deep down, we're afraid of what will happen if everything goes as planned.

If you achieve your Moonshot, everything changes. Your relationships change because you're operating at a different level. Your responsibilities change because success creates obligations. Your identity changes because you can no longer think of yourself as someone who's "aspiring" or "working toward" your Moonshot; you become someone who's achieved something brilliant.

Some of those changes are genuinely difficult. Success can create distance from people who knew you before. It can bring unwanted attention, increased pressure, and higher stakes. It can reveal that the goal itself wasn't actually what you wanted, but rather that it was the pursuit of the goal that gave your life structure (this is where serial entrepreneurs are born).

It is important to examine these fears honestly, because they are not without reason. Success does bring change, and not every change will feel comfortable at first. But here's what I've learned: the discomfort of success is qualitatively different from the discomfort of stagnation.

You may feel a sense of uneasiness when you transition into a different life after achieving success. You may look upon the days before with nostalgia. However, if you stay stagnant, you'll always wonder about what you could've been. Once again, the question from Chapter 9 comes to mind: "Could I have been anyone other than me?"

If you're afraid of success, examine what specifically you're afraid of. Write it down. Be specific. Are you afraid of losing relationships? Then commit to maintaining them deliberately; success doesn't destroy relationships, neglect does. Are you afraid of increased responsibility? Then build systems that can scale with your success rather than depending entirely on your personal effort. Are you afraid of becoming someone you don't recognize? Then anchor yourself to your values rather than your achievements. That's the whole point of defining your *Orbiting Ambition*.

Often, when you look closely at your fears of success, many of them begin to fade. What tends to remain is a fear of being seen — a fear of having your work and efforts visible to others, of stepping out from the safety of potential into the reality of action.

That fear is valid, but it's not a reason to stay hidden. Your work, your gifts, and your solutions to real problems don't help anyone while they're locked inside your head or trapped in cycles of endless preparation. The world doesn't need more people with potential. It needs more people willing to take action to make their potential a reality.

Fear of Permanence: The Commitment Trap

The third fear is far more subtle: the fear that choosing one Moonshot means foreclosing other options. This manifests as perpetual optionality, where you attempt to keep every door open, every path available, and every possibility alive by committing fully to nothing.

This may appear to be freedom, but in reality, it can become a kind of paralysis that masquerades as flexibility. By refusing to commit to a specific Moonshot, you may find that none of your options develop into something meaningful. It's like taking a broad college major that doesn't adequately prepare you for any career. It's like choosing to abstain from a meaningful vote because you are afraid of closing the door on the other option. Let me put it to you in the words of the musical Hamilton: "If you stand for nothing, what will you fall for?"

The irony is that true freedom of choice often comes from commitment, not from avoiding it. When you dedicate yourself to a Moonshot and make real progress, you build new skills, relationships, and resources that open doors you could not have imagined before. The person who completes a Moonshot often finds more genuine options available than the person who spent the same time keeping every possibility open but building nothing.

What the fear of permanence often hides is that choosing one path does not mean you can never change direction. Your Moonshot doesn't override the Lunar Cycle; it maximizes its utility. It's having the courage to chase something beyond your wildest dreams, and while it will change your life, it should do so for the better.

If you pursue a Moonshot and later realize it is not what you truly want, you can always adjust your course. The skills and insights you gain along the way remain with you, and the confidence that comes from attempting something challenging will stay, regardless of the outcome. The only way to remain truly stuck is to avoid choosing a direction altogether.

The Ignition Moment

Now you arrive at the point of ignition: the moment when preparation gives way to action, when intention transforms into commitment, and your Moonshot begins to take shape in reality.

Here's where things shift: I can't give you a system to decide when you're "ready" to take your Moonshot, because you will likely never feel completely ready for such a big leap. No one who has ever attempted something significant has felt fully prepared at the moment of launch. Most felt uncertain, underprepared, and keenly aware of everything that could go wrong.

They all, however, had one thing in common. Despite all of their uncertainty, they had the courage to launch anyway.

What I can share is that the ignition moment carries a distinct feeling. You will recognize it when it comes. It is the point when remaining where you are feels more difficult than stepping into the unknown. It is when the call of your *Orbiting Ambition* becomes stronger than the voice of your fear, and you realize that waiting longer will not make you more ready.

For me, the ignition moment for writing this book came after an ordinary evening drive. Nothing dramatic happened that told me I had to do it. I had simply been thinking about writing a book for years, and I had a brilliant idea for what this book could become. I woke up the next morning and realized that I was either going to do this or spend the rest of my life thinking about doing it; it was time for me to take the Moonshot.

Your ignition moment may be just as quiet. It might be sending an email, making a phone call, registering a domain, scheduling an appointment, submitting an application, or simply telling someone what you intend to do. It is the first small step that moves you from preparation into action.

The Legacy Question

As we come to a close, I invite you to consider a question that can help you move beyond fear, uncertainty, and hesitation around taking your Moonshot.

Imagine you're 90 years old. You're looking back on your life with full clarity about what you attempted and what you avoided. In that moment of honest accounting, what will you wish you'd done?

Will you wish you would've taken more risks or played it safer? Will you wish you would've attempted your Moonshot or stayed in your comfortable orbit? Will you wish you would've discovered what you were capable of or protected yourself from the possibility of failure?

I've never met anyone who reached the end of their life wishing they'd been more cautious about achieving their dreams. I've never heard anyone say they regret attempting something meaningful that didn't work out. However, I've heard countless people express deep regret about the things they didn't try, the dreams they never pursued, and the versions of themselves they never became because they were too afraid to take the first step.

If you wish to avoid that kind of regret, your Moonshot is not optional. It is not something to postpone until conditions are perfect, nor is it something you will ever feel completely ready for simply by waiting. It is the choice you are called to make now, with all your imperfections and uncertainties, or else risk carrying it as an unrealized possibility for the rest of your life.

The Final Truth

So, as clearly as I can express it, here is the final truth:

You are capable of more than you're currently doing. The Moonshot you're afraid to attempt is achievable. The version of yourself you can barely imagine becoming is already within you, waiting for permission to emerge.

That permission is not granted by anyone else. It does not arrive when circumstances are perfect, nor does it come from feeling completely ready or certain of success. It comes from you deciding that the life you want is worth the risk of pursuing it.

Everything you've learned in this book — the *Lunar Phase Framework*, the systems for building capabilities, and the strategies for navigating Tidal Forces and Lunar Eclipses — all become relevant only at the moment you actually commit to using them.

You can understand the framework perfectly and accomplish nothing if you never apply it to a real Moonshot. Or, you can apply it imperfectly to something that matters and transform the entire trajectory of your life.

You can decide the legacy that you want to leave behind, the impact you wish to have on others while you are here, and the fulfillment you feel from the work you do during your lifetime. The choice is yours, and it always has been.

Your bright, brilliant supermoon is there, hanging in your night sky, calling you to attempt something you've never done before. You can spend your life looking up at it, admiring it, imagining what it would be like to reach it. Or you can start building the systems, developing the capabilities, and taking the steps that will actually get you there.

Not someday. Not when you feel ready. Not when conditions improve.

Now.

Your future is waiting. The question is: will you find the courage to take your Moonshot?

Appendix

Acknowledgements

To my friends, family, and colleagues: thank you for standing beside me through every phase of this journey. Your encouragement, patience, and belief are what have helped give this book its gravity. Many of the stories, lessons, and principles within these pages were shaped by watching you live out your own forms of ambition, resilience, and purpose, and I am endlessly grateful for your love and support.

To every reader: thank you for giving your time, your attention, and your trust to this work. My hope is that the *Lunar Phase Framework for Success* will help you move closer to achieving your greatest goals, and that you continue to follow the pull of your own *Orbiting Ambition* long after these pages end.

References and Notes

The following references and notes provide the sources behind the ideas, studies, and case examples discussed throughout this book. Every effort has been made to include direct links to online materials where available; however, some web addresses may change or become inactive over time.

1 Psychology Today. (n.d.). *Hedonic treadmill.*
https://www.psychologytoday.com/us/basics/hedonic-treadmill
2 Collins, D. (2025, July 21). *Scottie Scheffler on how to take success in golf in stride.* ESPN. https://www.espn.com/golf/story/_/id/45745697/scottie-scheffler-take-success-golf-point
3 Hersh, M. (n.d.). *3 essential elements of genuine happiness.*
https://drmatthersh.com/3-essential-elements-of-genuine-happiness/
4 Patagonia. (n.d.). *How we got here: Organic cotton.*
https://www.patagonia.com/stories/how-we-got-here-organic-cotton/story-97024.html
5 Patagonia. (n.d.). *1% for the planet.* http://patagonia.com/one-percent-for-the-planet.html
6 Atlassian. (n.d.). *Waterfall methodology.*
https://www.atlassian.com/agile/project-management/waterfall-methodology
7 Atlassian. (n.d.). *Agile project management.* https://www.atlassian.com/agile
8 Startups.com. (n.d.). *Life after a startup exit: What comes next?*
https://www.startups.com/articles/life-after-startup-exit
9 Drehs, W. (2024, August 11). *The post-Olympic blues: Why some athletes feel empty after winning gold.* The New York Times / The Athletic.
https://www.nytimes.com/athletic/5650965/2024/08/11/post-olympic-blues-medal-depression/
10 Breuning, L. (2018, February). *The dopamine-seeking reward loop.* Psychology Today.
https://www.psychologytoday.com/us/blog/brain-wise/201802/the-dopamine-seeking-reward-loop202
11 Amabile, T. M., & Kramer, S. J. (2011). *The power of small wins.* Harvard Business School Working Knowledge.
https://www.hbs.edu/faculty/Pages/item.aspx?num=40692
12 Koo, M. (2009). *The Zeigarnik effect in everyday life.* PsycNET APA Record.
https://psycnet.apa.org/record/2009-12071-023

13 Psychology Today. (n.d.). *Zeigarnik effect.*
https://www.psychologytoday.com/us/basics/zeigarnik-effect
14 American Psychological Association. (n.d.). *Self-efficacy.*
https://www.apa.org/pi/aids/resources/education/self-efficacy
15 Clear, J. (n.d.). *2005 Stanford commencement address by Steve Jobs.*
https://jamesclear.com/great-speeches/2005-stanford-commencement-address-by-steve-jobs
16 Boogaard, K. (2023, December 26). *How to write SMART goals (with examples).*
Atlassian. https://www.atlassian.com/blog/productivity/how-to-write-smart-goals
17 Planning Fallacy Causes and Solutions. (n.d.). *Project Management Institute (PMI).* https://www.pmi.org/learning/library/planning-fallacy-causes-solutions-project-expectations-6374
18 Forbes Coaches Council. (2021, January 7). *How to incorporate realistic optimism into your life.* Forbes.
https://www.forbes.com/councils/forbescoachescouncil/2021/01/07/how-to-incorporate-realistic-optimism-into-your-life/
19 Clear, J. (n.d.). *Inversion: The mental model of avoiding stupidity.*
https://jamesclear.com/inversion
20 Foroux, D. (n.d.). *Skill stacking: The fastest way to become good at everything.*
https://dariusforoux.com/skill-stacking/
21 10X Growth Con. (n.d.). *Musicians who 10X'd their growth.*
https://10xgrowthcon.com/musicians-10x-growth-con/
22 Clear, J. (n.d.). *Stop procrastinating by using the Seinfeld strategy.*
https://jamesclear.com/stop-procrastinating-seinfeld-strategy
23 Clear, J. (n.d.). *You do not rise to the level of your goals; you fall to the level of your systems.* https://jamesclear.com/quotes/you-do-not-rise-to-the-level-of-your-goals-you-fall-to-the-level-of-your-systems
24 Peloton. (n.d.). *Habit stacking: The secret to sustainable change.*
https://www.onepeloton.com/blog/habit-stacking
25 Atlassian. (n.d.). *How to use time blocking to increase productivity.*
https://www.atlassian.com/blog/productivity/how-to-use-time-blocking
26 Clear, J. (n.d.). *The power of environment: Why context matters more than motivation.*
https://jamesclear.com/power-of-environment
27 American Psychological Association. (n.d.). *Willpower: A limited resource.*
https://www.apa.org/topics/willpower-limited.pdf203
28 Moran, G. (2024, August 14). *How to work more efficiently, according to a neuroscientist.* Fast Company. https://www.fastcompany.com/91191552/how-to-work-more-efficiently-according-a-neuroscientist
29 Schultz, W. (1997). *Predictive reward signal of dopamine neurons. Science, 275*(5306), 1593–1599. https://www.science.org/doi/abs/10.1126/science.275.5306.1593
30 Edwards, J. (2013, July 10). *The most extreme examples of secrecy at Apple. Business Insider.* https://www.businessinsider.com/the-most-extreme-examples-of-secrecy-at-apple-2013-7

31 NPR. (2018, March 26). *James Dyson on innovation and perseverance. National Public Radio.* https://www.npr.org/2018/03/26/584331881/dyson-james-dyson

32 Cleveland Clinic. (2023, June 2). *Dopamine: Functions, health effects, and disorders.* https://my.clevelandclinic.org/health/articles/22581-dopamine

33 Cleveland Clinic. (2023, May 11). *Serotonin: Functions and effects.* https://my.clevelandclinic.org/health/articles/22572-serotonin

34 Robertson, I. H. (2012). *The winner effect: The neuroscience of success and failure.* Thomas Dunne Books.

35 Cleveland Clinic. (2023, April 4). *Cortisol: What it is and how it affects your body.* https://my.clevelandclinic.org/health/articles/22187-cortisol

36 Acquired. (2015, October 12). *Episode 2: Instagram.* https://www.acquired.fm/episodes/episode-2-instagram

37 ProductPlan. (n.d.). *The 4 Ds of time management.* https://www.productplan.com/glossary/4-ds-of-time-management/

38 Fortune. (2023, April 14). *Netflix cofounder Marc Randolph recalls Blockbuster rejecting a chance to buy it. Fortune.* https://fortune.com/2023/04/14/netflix-cofounder-marc-randolph-recalls-blockbuster-rejecting-chance-to-buy-it/

39 Amazon. (n.d.). *About Amazon.* https://www.aboutamazon.com/about-us

40 National Center for Biotechnology Information. (2022). *Cortisol and stress responses. StatPearls Publishing.* https://www.ncbi.nlm.nih.gov/books/NBK585058/

41 Goodreads. (n.d.). *The best revenge is massive success (Frank Sinatra quote).* https://www.goodreads.com/quotes/46105-the-best-revenge-is-massive-success

42 "Formula for Leadership: Credibility = Competence + Trustworthiness." (2018, August 27). China Europe International Business School. https://www.ceibs.edu/new-papers-columns/formula-leadership-credibility-competence-trustworthiness

43 Cognitigence. (2024, June 3). *The architecture of influence: A deep dive into the principle of social proof.* https://www.cognitigence.com/blog/the-architecture-of-influence-a-deep-dive-into-the-principle-of-social-proof

44 Wharton Executive Education. (2021, July). *After action reviews: A simple tool for better teams.* https://executiveeducation.wharton.upenn.edu/thought-leadership/wharton-at-work/2021/07/after-action-reviews-simple-tool/

45 Dalio, R. (n.d.). *Principles: Life and work.* https://www.principles.com/principles/b1552e2e-f77b-46c0-b7dd-ba1f5c2b3407/204

46 Dalio, R. (n.d.). *Principles: Management and people.* https://www.principles.com/principles/a7c3050c-97d4-4011-ad8c-3852676e992b/

47 Su-Kubricht, L. P. (n.d.). *The 8 dimensions of wellness.* Rocky Mountain University. from https://rm.edu/blog/the-8-dimensions-of-wellness/

48 Centers for Disease Control and Prevention. (n.d.). *Module 3: Fatigue, long hours, and shift work.* https://www.cdc.gov/niosh/work-hour-training-for-nurses/longhours/mod3/08.html

49 Mayo Clinic Staff. (n.d.). *Exercise and stress: Get moving to manage stress. Mayo Clinic.* https://www.mayoclinic.org/healthy-lifestyle/stress-management/in-depth/exercise-and-stress/art-20044469

50 Acquired. (2015, October 28). *Episode 7: YouTube.* https://www.acquired.fm/episodes/episode-7-youtube

51 NBC News. (2006, October 5). *Apple's culture of secrecy. NBC News.* https://www.nbcnews.com/id/wbna15196982

52 NPR. (2018, July 27). *From Flickr to Slack: How Stewart Butterfield built two billion-dollar companies. National Public Radio.* https://www.npr.org/2018/07/27/633164558/slack-flickr-stewart-butterfield

53 Salesforce. (2020, December 1). *Salesforce signs definitive agreement to acquire Slack.* https://www.salesforce.com/news/press-releases/2020/12/01/salesforce-definitive-agreement-update/

54 Ibrahim, W. (2021, August 5). *Jeff Bezos uses a simple framework for making big decisions. Here's how it works.* Fast Company. https://www.fastcompany.com/90662406/jeff-bezos-uses-a-simple-framework-for-making-big-decisions-heres-how-it-works

About the Author

Hunter Hess is an award-winning entrepreneur and consultant who discovered the hard way that burnout isn't a badge of honor; it's a design flaw. After building multiple businesses, he developed the Lunar Phase Framework as a way to achieve ambitious goals without sacrificing health, relationships, or sanity.

He holds an MBA from Longwood University and a B.S. in Management Information Systems from the University of Virginia's College at Wise. Based in Virginia, Hess writes and speaks about ambition, balance, and the systems that make lasting success possible.

www.ingramcontent.com/pod-product-compliance
Lightning Source LLC
Chambersburg PA
CBHW071157130626
46553CB00004B/1700